Library of
Davidson College

The Aftermath

A SURVIVOR'S ODYSSEY THROUGH
WAR-TORN EUROPE

The Aftermath

A SURVIVOR'S ODYSSEY THROUGH WAR-TORN EUROPE

HENRY LILIENHEIM

DC BOOKS, Montréal
In association with

Cover design by Gerald Luxton
based on a concept by Henry Lilienheim.

Designed and typeset in Times by DCAD Enterprises, Montreal.

Printed and bound in Canada by Les Editions Marquis Ltée.

Copyright © Henry Lilienheim, 1994.

Dépot légal, Bibliothèque nationale du Québec
and the National Library of Canada, 4th trimester, 1994.

Canadian Cataloguing in Publication Data.

Lilienheim, Henry, 1908—
The Aftermath: a survivor's odyssey through war-torn Europe

ISBN 0-919688-45-4 (bound) —
ISBN 0-919688-44-6 (pbk.)

1. Lilienheim, Henry, 1908- . 2. Holocaust survivors—Poland—Biography. 3. Jews—Poland—Biography. 4. Holocaust survivors—United States—Biography. 5. Holocaust, Jewish (1939-1945)—Personal narratives. 6. Jews—United States—Biography. I. Title.

D811.5.L54A3 1994   940.53'18'092   C94-900585-1

Publisher:
DC Books, 1495 rue de l'Eglise, Box 662, Montreal, Que., H4L 4V9

To the memory of my parents and family,
and to Lydia, Michael and Irene.

Acknowledgments

MANY HEARTFELT THANKS to my daughter, Irene, without whom this book would never have appeared. A few years ago she discovered an old manuscript which I had written in 1947. The manuscript inspired her to make her film, *Dark Lullabies,* based partially on my experiences and search for my wife. The film, co-directed with her husband, Abbey Neidik, won first prizes in festivals in many countries. She then went on to pursue the publication of the manuscript. Irene's editorial skill and dedication improved the book in great measure. Irene, I love you for being Irene, and for all your help.

I was also assisted by the advice and talent of my son-in-law whose artistic sensitivity greatly helped in editing the manuscript and substantially improving its structure.

My son, Michael, by his empathy and warm understanding, was an inspiration and encouragement while I was rewriting the book.

I owe a debt of deep gratitude to my editor, Mark Pendergrast, who first insisted that the manuscript should be published. His commitment, intelligence and literary gifts contributed invaluably to the book.

My publisher, Steve Luxton, with his poet's vision, provided meaningful advice.

Thanks also to Naomi Kramer for her meticulous checking of historical facts.

Most of all, I thank my wife, Lydia. Her patience and understanding made it possible for me to write, both in 1947 and today. And she enriched the manuscript greatly by her vivid description of her camp experiences. Thank you for everything, Lydia. You always amaze me!

Contents

Acknowledgments — ix
Foreword — xiii
Maps — xix
Liberation — 1
The River — 9
The Dance Hall — 18
Denazification — 24
Flight — 32
The Search — 42
Hope — 48
Escape Plans — 53
Liquidation — 60
The Ruins of Warsaw — 66
Estonia — 79
Only Two Remain — 89
Writings — 94
One Morning — 100
Prontosil — 114
Marek Dworzecki — 121
Marseilles — 127
Zionism — 132
The Germans — 138

The Letter — 145
United — 146
Lydia's Story — 151
The Album — 161
Homelessness — 165
Kaddish — 168
Birth — 170
Afterword — 173
About the author — 181

Foreword

MY FATHER SAT DOWN to write this book a year after his liberation from Dachau, the year that I was born. It would be another twenty-five years before he gave me the manuscript which he had written in part for me. And it would be another several years before I dared to read it. Yet it seems that I have always known my parents' incredible story, even though I marvel, again, every time I read it.

My mother decided when I was born that I should grow up as a happy, normal child, free from any thoughts of the horrors they had experienced in the Holocaust. My father did not entirely agree that I should not be told anything, though he went along with her decision. But the Holocaust was too large for even my mother to hide, and she could not prevent me from occasionally overhearing little bits of conversation between them, or with their many Survivor friends. Nor could she spare me from the emotions about the Holocaust that I, like most children of Survivors, absorbed by some form of osmosis as I was growing up.

Still, it was a happy childhood, filled with love and laughter. My parents were able to get out of Germany when I was two and a half, and we came to the United States — land of the liberators, land of freedom. In America, they created a new family for my brother, Michael, and me, made up of friends, many of them Survivors, who filled in as "aunts," "uncles" and "cousins." We met on Sundays for dinners and picnics, and spent summer months together in the country. I did not realize that no one of our own family was alive. I did wonder why the other kids had grandparents, and what had happened to mine. But by that time I was not asking about the Holocaust.

The Holocaust was a forbidden subject. Even as a young adult, I did not discuss it, did not read about it, even left the cinema if I inadvertently found myself watching a film about the subject. This was not indifference. Rather, my feelings about the Holocaust were so intense that I was not able to deal with them. The Holocaust was burning inside me.

One day, after I had begun my career as a filmmaker, I was invited by my producer to meet Marcel Ophuls and screen his films. As usual, I refused, explaining that I found it too painful to watch films about the Holocaust. Nevertheless, a week later, I found myself in the theatre watching an interview with Albert Speer, Reich Minister of Armaments, in Ophul's film, *Memory of Justice*.

That interview jolted my consciousness. For the first time, I realized that those who had caused so much suffering and horror were not all easily identifiable monsters, but people who appeared to possess normal human qualities. This gave rise to a flood of questions, and I felt a responsibility to find out what had happened and why. I began to explore, very carefully, the landscape I had avoided for thirty years. I already had the manuscript my father had written. It had been waiting on my bookshelf, never opened. With great trepidation, I began to read.

What I read amazed me. This was not just a story of horror and grief, as I had expected, but a powerful and moving story of love and hope, as well. Its scope was as vast as the greatest tragedy in human history, and as intimate as a man's unswerving search for his wife after a journey through Hell.

Once I began reading, I could not stop.

Thus began my journey back to Dachau to try to understand the legacy I inherited. The questions my father struggled with in this book gave birth to my own — questions about love and hate, prejudice and justice, inhumanity and courage, questions about decisions. Not just decisions made by people in power, but those made by ordinary citizens — decisions to follow orders, to turn a blind eye, to ignore the voice of conscience within.

Being a filmmaker, I made my journey on film. With my husband, Abbey Neidik, I co-directed and produced *Dark Lullabies*, the story of the next generation. The manuscript that my father wrote was my constant guide and inspiration.

Abbey and I interviewed children of Survivors in Canada, the United States and Israel. They became part of my extended family, and Israel became a second home. In Germany, we met children of Nazis and other second generation Germans, including a fellow filmmaker, Harald Lüders, who led us into a world I thought I would never enter — the world of the perpetrators. In trying to understand what had happened, I had crossed over an abyss.

Dark Lullabies did very well, winning prizes and filling theatres worldwide. People were especially moved by the lines from my father's manuscript cited in the opening and closing of the film, and many asked about reading the book. We realized then that *The Aftermath* must be published. Mark Pendergrast, a wonderful writer who later became a dear friend, came to a screening to review the film. He became the prime motivator of this effort, and we will always be grateful to him. Steve Luxton of DC Books jumped at the chance to publish it and, so, after forty-seven years, *The Aftermath* was finally reaching print.

First there was editing to do, material to add, and some smoothing out of the language. My father has mastered nine languages in his life. He chose to write the manuscript in English, his fourth language, even though he was living in Germany at the time. He and my mother were determined to raise their family in America, and he wanted the manuscript to be read in what would become our native tongue.

Over the years, my father had written several additional stories he wanted to include. Abbey, who is so good at structuring films, made some valuable suggestions for the structure of the new, expanded version of the book. Mark brought his creative touch to all the writing, and interviewed my mother with exceptional sensitivity. My mother's chapter is included in *The Aftermath* almost verbatim as she told it for the first time. It is moving and powerful and beautifully described. I had my hands on everything, working with obsessive passion on this creation of a lifetime.

Sometimes, as I worked, I longed to reach back and save all those we lost in the Holocaust, to protect my parents from the unspeakable horrors they faced. The past, unfortunately, cannot be undone. But by facing our history, I believe we can understand the forces that allowed the Holocaust to happen and, in its shadow, begin to create a world rich in meaning and tolerance for everyone.

The Aftermath begins on the eve of the liberation of Dachau and recounts the compelling events in the months that followed. It reveals the courage of the Survivors to rebuild their lives with strength and hope, and to give birth again to their dreams, even after that journey through Hell.

Out of so much hatred, my father wrote a love story. And this is my legacy. Love for all people of goodwill, as my grandmother used to say at her Friday night prayers for Shabbat; love for my family; love for my parents — my heroes.

This book set me on a journey years ago. Now yours is about to begin. I hope that in reading *The Aftermath,* you too will discover the humanity, courage and love that I did. *Shalom.* Peace.

Irene Lilienheim Angelico

Montreal, 1994.

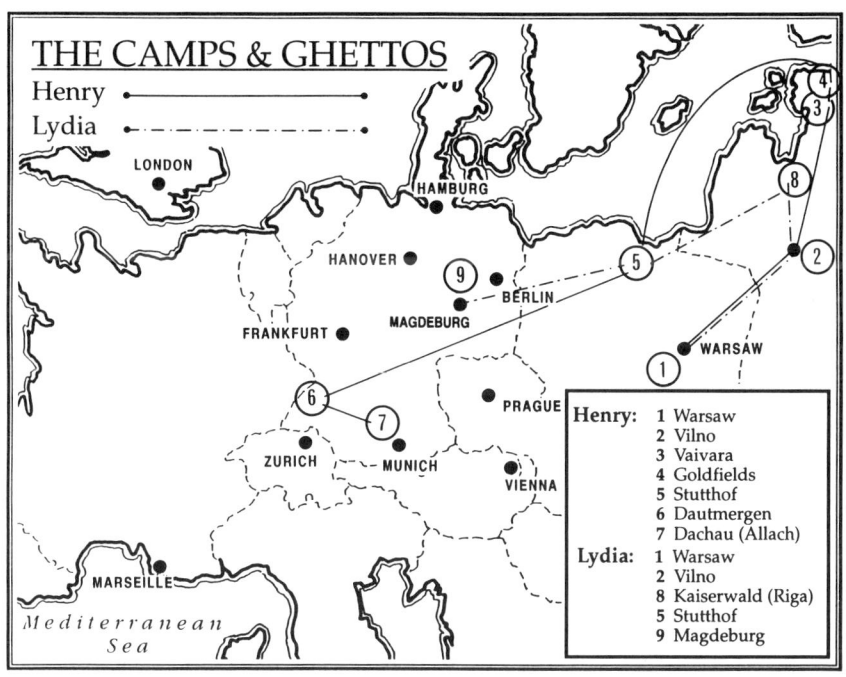

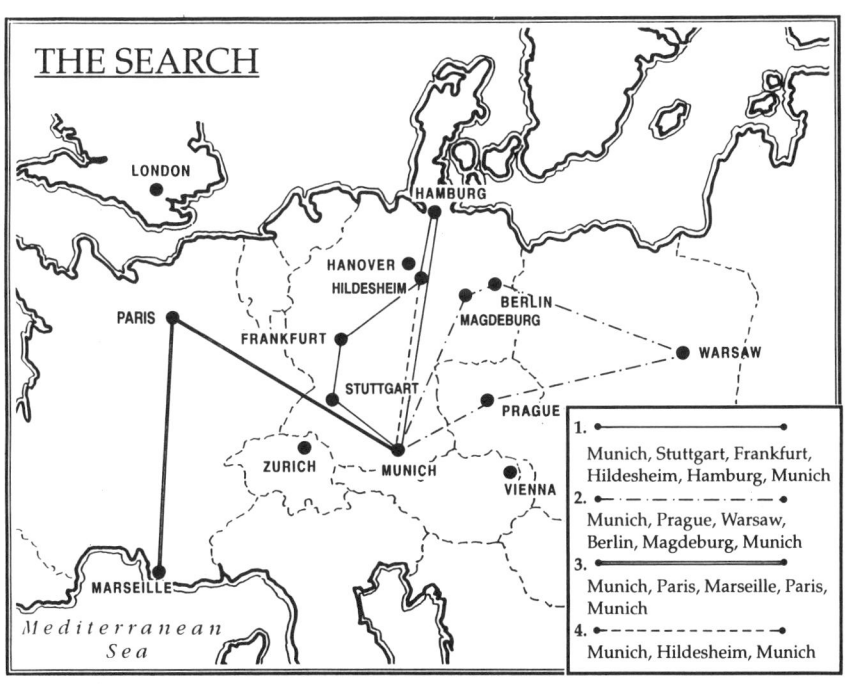

The Aftermath
A SURVIVOR'S ODYSSEY THROUGH WAR-TORN EUROPE

Liberation

RA-TATATA-TA. Ra-tatata-ta. The growl of machine guns. From time to time the distant roar of cannons. I am lying on the third tier of a bed of boards. I am cold. I have covered my head with a blanket. I think of food and then, with indifference, I realize that this is perhaps the last day of my slavery, or of my life. Have only four years passed?

I am in the concentration camp Allach, a branch of Dachau, several kilometers from Munich. What date is it today? The night of the 29th of April, 1945. Will I be a free man tomorrow? I do not know; I am tired of thinking. All I want is not to be hungry.

Suddenly, a long whistle, then an explosion. A shell hits the camp "hospital" where I am lying. Screams and cries. I raise my blanket and look to the right. Five meters away where, a moment ago, people were lying in rows of bunks, there is only a heap of rubbish.

All around me, confusion and yelling. I cover my head again and think. I have almost made it to the shore. Every day for four years I have fought to keep my head above the raging waves of this flood of cruelty. A thousand times I thought I would drown. If I have to be drowned, what a pity it did not happen in the beginning, what a pity that this tremendous effort has been in vain. Yet I can hardly do anything more. Just a step separates me from the shore, but there is nothing to grab onto. I have to wait. Either the next wave will throw me onto shore, or the water will swallow me forever.

Ra-tatata-ta. Ra-tatata-ta....

"Listen." I hear Milnok's voice. He is lying on my left. "Tomorrow we will be either dead or free. I want to live. You know how I've struggled for life. A hundred times a day. If we survive, I will travel around the world. I will tell the people everywhere what happened to us. I am weak now, but I have an iron will. Henryk! You saved my life. You are my only friend. The only man in the world I love. If we are free tomorrow, don't abandon me. I will rest a while, and we will try to reach Vilno. I buried a treasure there in the cellar of a factory. Even if the factory has been bombed, I will remember where it is buried, under a stone in the floor. We will be rich. We will go to New York, Melbourne, Rio de Janeiro. We will tell the world of the hell we left so that such a hell will never again appear on this earth. I want to live, Henryk! Oh, how I love life. I want to live!"

Milnok speaks in a staccato voice without moving his head. Only his eyes turn towards me, burning feverishly. The once stocky man with a solid physique now lies emaciated and weak. He has been lying like this for a week. I take care of him. When we get soup, I feed him with a spoon. When he has to go down — which is often — I put his body on my back and carry him down the three tiers to the floor. I place him on the edge of a large tub in the middle of the hall. The tub is always so full that excrement overflows and is spread by our bare feet through the room and onto the beds. Someone entering our room for the first time would be shocked and repulsed by the stench of excrement and urine and corpses. To us, it is quite normal.

The room is big and dark and has a few small windows. Two rows of wooden bunks are stacked three tiers high. On the bunks the camp inmates lie covered with grey blankets. Emaciated, haggard faces, eyes staring with glazed incomprehension. At the rear of the barrack, corpses are heaped one on top of another, a mountain of desiccated legs and arms, ghastly eyes, gaping mouths.

I look down. Rubbish is being taken away and the wounded carried out. "Don't get excited," I tell Milnok. "Hang on. You'll be free in a few hours. I'll take care of you until you regain your strength. We'll leave the camp and head West. We'll try to reach Paris. Some organizations will surely help us find those of our families who survived."

The firing stops. Silence. Is it possible that we are free? Is it possible that life will no longer mean suffering, hunger, filth? It seems so natural to suffer, to be hungry, to see people dying around you, to know that you too can die any day. Could it ever be different?

Silence. From time to time someone moans. I fall asleep.

Something wakes me up. The pale light of a grey, gloomy dawn filters through small windows. The sound of people running. I hear voices. "The Americans? They are here? We are free!" People embrace and kiss each other, weeping. I wrap myself with my thin blanket. Trembling with cold, I leave the barracks. I try to run through the camp to the entrance gate, but I am weak and have to stop to catch my breath. I tell myself, "You are free. You are free. Do you understand? You survived. Today, on this cold, grey day, a miracle has happened." But I cannot comprehend my freedom. Perhaps I am so weak that I am hallucinating.

The Aftermath

Near the gate a crowd of crying and gesticulating inmates. In the middle, two soldiers with rifles. They wear helmets and strange-looking shoes. So these are Americans. They really exist? Four years we read and talked about them, and now they are here. I force my way through the crowd until I reach one of the soldiers. I kiss his helmet and his cheeks. Tears flow from my eyes for the first time in four years. The young soldier smiles, takes a bar of chocolate from his pocket and gives it to me. I am unable to say a word. I turn and go back to the barracks.

A banner of stars and stripes flutters on the roof of the barracks. On the road outside the camp's fences, rows of cars with smiling soldiers make their way into the camp. Liberators!

In the barracks, people show each other cans of food the Americans have given them. The cans are of different shapes and sizes with bright colored labels showing pictures of fat cows and fish and fruit.

A young Russian embraces me. "Brother. We are free!"

I climb up to the third tier, to my bed of boards. "Milnok, we are free!" His eyes gleam.

I lie down, tired but excited. One of the inmates, a young Norwegian, comes in to tell us that we will get bigger rations. We are given half a kilogram of bread instead of the usual one hundred and fifty grams, and a bowl of thick, nourishing soup. The soup and bread are the first tangible proofs of freedom. We are not aware of the strain on our weakened stomachs, and we eat all the soup and bread we are given. The results are disastrous. I have to take Milnok down. The tub is surrounded by people. We already suffer from chronic dysentery, but within a few hours our reaction to more food becomes critical.

We cannot understand that we are free. The Germans and the hunger have vanished, but we are still in the same filthy barracks. Our stomachs are full, but our eyes are hungry for more food. The first joy of freedom is mixed with the pain in our stomachs.

Milnok's condition becomes worse. I bring him down almost every hour, till my muscles falter and I finally give up. He is lying in his excrement. Again, we receive half a kilogram of bread and a thick soup. Milnok does not eat this time; only his eyes are fixed on the rations. Although I know how risky it is, I swallow my whole share.

Within forty-eight hours, more people are dying each day than before the liberation.

Milnok says something. I come near him. In a barely audible voice he whispers, "I am dying. I want to live. What a pity to die now." He fixes his eyes on me. His look becomes glassy. "Milnok," I cry out, "you must live. Do you hear me? You must live!"

His eyes have a fixed gaze. I touch his arm. It does not move. I turn his face away; I cannot endure the sight of his eyes. Something strangles my throat. I have seen death hundreds of times and I thought I was inured to the sight of it, but now, after liberation, it is different.

I cover his face with a blanket. I take my blanket and go down from the bed. A young Italian on the lower bunk is holding his stomach with both hands, crying from pain. I climb up to find some other free space. I lie down and look at the ceiling for a long time.

"Don't worry, you fool," the neighbor on my left says in Russian. "We are free. We will soon eat sausage and *borscht* and cabbage soup. The soil in Kuban is fertile, and there is plenty of everything. My wife knows how to cook. A year from now, you won't recognize Ivan Kusnetsov. Come and visit me there. You'll get plenty to eat, drink and smoke, too."

I look at Kusnetsov's broad Russian face. He has pale blue eyes, a bulbous nose, flaxen short-cropped hair and stubble on his cheeks. "I was a soldier in the Red Army," he says. "Our regiment was stationed in Noworossijsk and we were ordered to Crimea. Once we landed, we advanced a short stretch from the shore. And then it happened. We were surrounded. Only a few managed to escape and run back to the ships. The rest of us were taken prisoner and sent to a camp. I've been in many prisons and camps. So many of us died of hunger or exhaustion, but I survived."

Ivan Kusnetsov likes to talk. I listen to his stories and try not to think of Milnok's death. Days pass, and Kusnetsov talks on and on.

A quarantine is declared because of typhus. We are forbidden to leave the camp until it is over. The camp is surrounded by American sentries. They are supposed to enforce the quarantine, but some enterprising inmates succeed in escaping during the night.

Most of us are too weak to think of escaping. We are afflicted with severe dysentery, and a few people die every day. Will we survive another week? I think about escaping from the camp but, without food or clothes and not knowing where to go, I resign myself to lying on my bunk, suffering diarrhea, and listening to Kusnetsov's stories. After a week, the portions of thick soup are reduced and we are a bit hungry again, but the crisis of acute dysentery subsides.

Another week, and the first transports of people leave the camp. First the Frenchmen, then the Italians, the Dutch, and the Czechs. They have homes to return to. Only large groups of Poles, Yugoslavs, Jews, and a few other groups still remain.

Two weeks after liberation, field showers are installed in a meadow near the camp. Our old clothes and blankets are thrown onto a pile. A black soldier sprays us with powder and each of us gets a collarless shirt, drawers, socks, a green uniform, and a pair of heavy German military shoes.

Days without joy. Where is our freedom? Barbed wires still surround us. We are weak and in a stupor. How do we begin life again? Will someone or something from the outside world show us the way? We wait for orders telling us where to go and what to do. Only the German guards and the heaps of corpses have disappeared. Nothing else has really changed. We face the same grey camp landscape.

Three weeks after liberation, the quarantine is still in force. I want to leave the camp and come up with a plan. The war with Germany is over, but the war in Asia is still on. Some years ago I studied the Chinese language. With effort, I could refresh my knowledge of it. Possibly this may be useful to the Americans. I write a letter to the American commander of the camp offering my services, and ask a GI at the camp gate to deliver it to the captain.

The following morning, I am called to the camp office. A short, rotund major and a tall captain, both in smart uniforms, ask me various questions. Finally, they tell me that I will not go to the East to work, but since I know English and German fairly well, I will go to Munich. A car will come in the afternoon to take me there. In the meantime, if I wish, I am free to take a walk outside the camp. The captain gives me a piece of paper. A pass.

I show the pass to the American sentry and walk through the gate of the camp. I walk slowly along a road about a kilometer. Everything appears unreal. I see a hill with trees not far from the highway. I turn into the field.

Lilac trees are flowering. I pluck a leaf of elder and suck on the sweet stalk. I spread my jacket under a tree and lie down on it. The rays of the sun filter through the leaves and cast golden spots on the soft red moss. An ant runs onto my hand. As it comes to the end of my finger, I bring the nail of another finger to form a bridge, and the ant runs across. When I drop the ant to the ground, it seizes a crumb and runs ahead.

Suddenly the ant turns aside, as a large grasshopper jumps in front of it. If not for this jump, I would never have noticed the well camouflaged leaper among the green grass and moss. The stalk from which it jumped is still trembling when a yellow field butterfly comes to rest on the leaf. It stops fluttering its speckled wings and gently folds them together. Its tiny antennae vibrate in the sunlight. A fly stubbornly buzzes around my head. Warm rays of sun wash my face. I inhale the heady aroma of lilac. My lungs are filled with the ambrosia. How sweet it is to be alive! The past is a horrible nightmare, and now I am awake. Reality is this moment, the scent of the lilacs, the clouds drifting in the sky, the softness of the moss.

Yet something is missing. Someone. Lydia should be lying by my side, sharing this joy with me. Could she, with her indomitable will, have survived the atrocities? Is it possible that at this very moment she is lying under another lilac tree in a field somewhere?

The River

I RETURN to the camp. After a long good-bye to Kusnetsov and a few other inmates, I walk once more out the gate to a car where a lieutenant and his driver wait for me. We reach Munich in some twenty minutes, a world away from Dachau. We drive along an elegant street flanked by fine buildings. "Prinzregentenstrasse," the driver says. "In front of you is the monument of the Angel of Peace."

We cross a bridge over a green-colored river and turn onto a quiet street. "Here we are," says the driver, "Holbein Strasse." On the front wall of the building is a sign with a shield in red, white and blue: "Office of the U.S. Military Government of Bavaria."

"You'll start working tomorrow, Henry," Colonel Quirk says as he greets me. He speaks in a gravely voice. He is a tall, hulking man with thick grey eyebrows above a prominent nose. I am sure he has spent his life as a professional military man. He commands immediate respect, but there is something sad about him that calls forth sympathy as well. His rugged appearance and gruff voice hide a gentle manner. "How long have you been in the camps?"

"Four years, sir."

He takes this in for a moment. I can see him pondering what this might mean to the man standing in front of him.

Then he brushes the thought aside. "So, you begin a new life. We are organizing the Denazification Branch of the Military Government. There are three Americans here and three Germans. You will be the first DP."

"Beg your pardon, sir?"

"You will be the first DP here. Displaced person."

So that is what I must learn to call myself. "DP." Initials which stand for a lost human being, lacking any proper place. It sounds so impersonal, like a carelessly handled household item. A misplaced boot. A displaced person.

"Well, we'll expect you here at work tomorrow. But now, I would advise you to report to Captain McDonald, the officer in charge of DPs. He will inform you about your lodging. His office is in the city hall in downtown Munich."

"Thank you, sir. I will go right there."

"Okay, young man. See you tomorrow."

I walk down Prinzregentenstrasse. People in the street stare at me. I probably appear strange to them, and perhaps older than my thirty-seven years. I walk haltingly, out of practice and weak from my time in the camps. I am wearing a green uniform, a collarless shirt, and heavy military shoes. My clothes hang loosely on my body. My hair is cropped. I hold a canteen with a piece of bread in it. This is all I possess.

At the end of the street, I turn toward Odeonplatz. Standing in the square, I recall a photograph I once saw in the paper, a scene from 1914. A crowd was standing in this very square in front of the Feldherrnhalle monument, rejoicing at the declaration of war. Hitler was in the crowd waving his hat with frantic enthusiasm. That was thirty-one years ago. Now the monument looms grandly before me, a Teutonic figure flanked by two lions. Someone has painted big white letters on the base of the monument: "*Ich schäme mich ein Deutscher zu sein.* I am ashamed to be a German."

I continue on my way and soon come to the Munich Rathaus, City Hall, with its figure of a little monk, the patron of Munich, looking over the city. I enter Captain McDonald's office.

"I can't help you," a slender young woman in military uniform tells me, looking up for a moment from her paperback novel. "The captain's not in." She goes back to her book. I continue to stand there, so she looks up again. "And even if he were, he wouldn't be able to help, either. There's still no organized place for DPs in Munich. You're the first DP to come to this office."

I tell her I have just left a concentration camp that morning. I ask if she has any suggestions. "What nationality are you?" she asks. "I can't tell one accent from another around here." Learning that I am Polish, she suggests I try the Polish Committee in the German Museum.

I am beginning to tire of trudging through this city. It is a depressing place, a mixture of bombed-out buildings, rubble, and surviving monuments to former German greatness. No one knows what to do with me. I feel a stranger in a strange land. I reach the museum in half an hour. It is an immense building, partly in ruins, standing on an island in the middle of the Isar River.

"We have no place for you," a Polish secretary tells me. She seems even less friendly than the American woman. "We've only been here a few days, and the three or four beds we have are occupied. You'll have to go outside Munich."

A young Pole standing nearby overhears our conversation. "This man has just come from a camp," he interjects. "He must be exhausted. Give him my place at the German Museum. I can arrange to stay with friends." He is a slim, blond young man with a gentle face and lively blue eyes.

"My name is Leo. I'm sure you're hungry. Let's go some place to eat."

Over a simple meal of bread and soup, he tells me of his experience during the war. An able-bodied non-Jewish Pole, he was brought to Germany as a *"Fremdarbeiter,* a forced laborer." "I really have nothing to complain about," he says. "I was not starved or beaten or put into a camp like you." I am grateful to him for the food. Later, he shows me the room he is giving up for me. I am almost too tired to thank him. I am half asleep before I fall onto the cot.

Next morning I get up early and head towards the Office of the Military Government. On my way, I notice a gate leading into a small garden with a sign in oblique golden letters for the brewery next door: *"Buergerbraeukeller."* Cars and trucks of the American Red Cross are parked in the garden. This is where the Nazi movement started, I think, and now I am walking quietly by it.

A friendly young American in a dapper uniform welcomes me in the office on Holbein Strasse. "I'm Sergeant Garety," he says, jumping up to shake my hand. He speaks and moves very quickly. "Call me Garety. Cigarette? You don't smoke? Here's some gum. You haven't shaved. Tomorrow I'll bring you a shaving kit and whatever else I can get for you. One step at a time. Now, about your job. See this pile of *Kraut Fragebogen?"*

"Excuse me. What do you mean, Garety?"

"Kraut, you know, German. These are questionnaires. Read each one and make a summary. I mean, write down the most important points. We just need a summary of all of them. Don't ask me why. I already know what the bastards did. None of 'em will tell the truth about it, anyhow." He gives me a pile of papers and shows me where I will

work. Garety is a little overwhelming at first, but his energy and frankness appeal to me. I like him.

I find the work interesting. I go over each file, checking some hundred answers on each. They have asked the obvious questions. Were you a member of the Party? If so, what year did you enlist? Did you inform on your neighbors? Some of the files are of prominent Bavarian Nazis whose names I recall from newspapers. Sergeant Garety was right. Unless they are caught in a lie, most of them say how they had no choice but to follow orders. They joined the Nazis unwillingly, because they had to. None of them ever informed on anyone or personally hurt a Jew.

"How are you doing, young man?" I hear Colonel Quirk's husky voice. "You seem to like the work. Are you on the payroll already?"

"On what, sir?"

"On the payroll. The list of salaries. You need to improve your English. Have you ever been in the States?"

"No, sir, I've been only in England."

"That's all right. You'll learn fast. Here's a parcel for you, just a few things you might need."

"Thank you so much, sir."

I feel grateful to the Americans. They liberated me, and now they are helping me start a new life. If not for their sweat and blood, I would have died in the camps. This nation produced Abraham Lincoln, whose speeches I once memorized. His words stand out in my mind. "As I would not be a slave, so I would not be a master. Whatever differs from this, to the extent of difference, is no democracy."

A while later, Sergeant Garety leads two men and a woman to my desk. "I want you to meet your colleagues," he says. "They work with us here. This is Herr Raff, Fräulein Gertrud, and Herr Wagner."

The Aftermath

A wave of involuntary anger rushes through me at the mere sound of their names. "This is Henry Lilienheim," Garety continues, "a survivor of the concentration camps."

"I am glad to meet you," says Herr Raff, a lanky man with a high forehead and deep-set eyes. He extends his hand. For a moment, I am uncertain if I should shake it, but then I do. "I will try to convince you that not all Germans are bad," he adds.

I do not know how to react. There is an awkward silence. Finally, I say, "I never thought that all Germans were bad, Herr Raff, but I definitely believe that most Germans are guilty, at least of indifference."

He nods. "Yes, I must agree with you."

"And I cannot," interjects Herr Wagner. "Many of us were against the Nazis, those scoundrels." I stare at the short, balding man with his fat cheeks and large, slightly protruding eyes. An obsequious smile is pasted on his face. His words have the same false ring I have been detecting in some of the answers to the questionnaires. He's not to be trusted, I think. Fräulein Gertrud, a stern middle-aged woman in a black dress, does not say anything. She nods slightly in acknowledgement of Herr Wagner's statement, and smiles tightly with pursed lips.

After work, I return to the German Museum and find the huge building completely empty. Puzzled, I walk along the endless corridors until, finally, I see someone standing in the corner of a big hall. He approaches me, a pale, nervous, tired-looking man of about forty, wearing a shabby suit. "I am Doctor Ordecki," he introduces himself. "I know who you are. Leo told me. The Polish Committee moved this morning to a suburb of Munich. We are the only two left here. I didn't go because I've already set up my office and some laboratory equipment in one of the rooms. And you? Have you anywhere else to go?"

"No, Doctor, I don't. This is only my second day in Munich."

"So many rooms here. Why don't you choose one? Come. Let us first have a snack in my room. We'll chat about Poland."

"With pleasure. I was getting hungry and I had no idea where to eat."

As Doctor Ordecki prepares some cold cuts, he tells me about his war experiences. He was an officer in General Anders' army of volunteer Polish exiles which was attached to the Allies. He fought at Monte Cassino, where the bravery of the Poles contributed greatly to opening the way to Rome for General Clark. Ordecki was captured by the Germans and sent to a camp for prisoners in Murnau in Bavaria. After liberation, he came to Munich. He has since learned that all of his family — his parents, a brother and sister — perished in Warsaw. I try to console him, but what can I say? I too have lost my loved ones. After some conversation, we eat in silence.

After the meal, I search the wide corridors of the German Museum to choose a room. I settle on a small room that seems the most pleasant. It has simple furniture — a table, two chairs, a chest of drawers, and a military cot with a straw mattress. The window is just above the Isar River. As I gaze out, I am struck by the fine green color of the river. Its constant roar is soothing to my ears.

I unpack the gift from Colonel Quirk. What treasures! These are things I can call mine. A few shirts, a towel, some soap. Some things I still badly miss, but this is a good start. And what a delight it will be to sleep alone in the room, not to hear voices cursing, crying, moaning, not to worry about the relentless calamities that the next day may bring.

Night has fallen. I look out the window at the shimmering stars. I listen to the roar of the river. "I am nature. I am God," it seems to say. "I am part of a great mystery that you can never understand. You were a slave yesterday. Today you are free. You have suffered beyond the limits of endurance, but you have survived. When you look at the stars, understand that all this is part of the eternal order."

Yes, I think, but I cannot help asking why all this has happened. "If you are a part of God," I ask the river, "tell me why? Why did all this happen to me?"

"Do you believe in God?" the river is asking.

"I do not know. The question has tormented me for a long time. Nothing proves to me that He exists, and nothing proves that He does not. I have seen death a thousand times. Someone speaks and his soul is reflected in his words. Then he speaks no more. His eyes are glassy and his hands cold. What happens to his soul when he dies? I have seen scenes of great cruelty, injustices that went unpunished. I have seen good, innocent people tortured and murdered, children killed in front of their mothers' eyes. Where was God then?"

The river answers, "You speak like someone who is looking up at the sky on a stormy, winter day. You see the dark, threatening clouds and think that there is nothing more. But then, on a clear night in May, you look up and see a thousand bright stars, and realize that there are millions more you cannot see. Think of your mother. Do you remember her gentle, grey eyes? Can you hear her voice? You know she is no longer alive, but do you believe she no longer exists? Was she only a flame in a black night of eternity, a flame which flashed and went out? Do you believe that you will never see her again?"

"No, I can't believe that. Tell me, tell me, will I ever see her again?"

"I cannot tell you that. And I cannot explain what has happened to you. But listen to your soul. Even if you do not understand this world, if you can hear your soul speak to you, you can believe in God."

The river is roaring, roaring. I stare into the waves. I see the face of my mother, and one by one, the faces of everyone I loved. Of all of them, I know that only my wife, Lydia, could have survived.

I fall asleep in the small room by the river.

The Dance Hall

THE NEXT FEW DAYS bring joys that might seem insignificant to those leading ordinary lives. What a luxury it is, after so many years, to plunge into a bathtub for the first time. What a delight to wear a clean shirt, to go to a barber's shop and feel my smooth skin after a shave. Do people know how to enjoy their lives, to appreciate everyday comforts? Is it necessary to return from hell to take pleasure in the small things most people take for granted? I enjoy going to the movies, reading newspapers and magazines, and learning what is happening in the world. The newspapers are full of beautiful words. Liberty. Democracy. Goodwill Among Nations. The Four Freedoms.

Above all, it is so good to feel free, to go where I want and do what I want. To be alone, if I choose. Not to feel hunger, cold or fatigue. To shake off the constant awareness that death is just a step behind.

After a few days, the once empty rooms of the German Museum swarm with people. First arrivals are men and women in smart American uniforms with UNRRA badges on their arms. "What do the letters UNRRA mean?" I ask one woman. "It's the United Nations Relief and Rehabilitation Administration," she answers. Relief? I think. Yes, perhaps. But rehabilitation? I wonder if that is possible.

Workers arrive to remove rubbish from the cavernous halls. Within a few weeks, various organizations open offices, and every day hundreds of people arrive to find transient lodging, assistance and advice. A special newspaper for displaced persons is printed and distributed. A big coffee house with space for dancing opens in the building.

Munich has become an important gathering point for the displaced persons of Europe, and the German Museum lies at the crossroads. DPs converge here on their way east or west, north or south. Many still remain behind the barbed wires of former Nazi camps, but gradually the camps are being liquidated. The former camp inmates mix with the masses of forced laborers who worked in factories or on farms. The dying has ended. The supply of food from UNRRA is adequate. Faces which were emaciated with hunger a month before recover their normal look. I look at myself in a small mirror the Americans gave me and see my face almost as I remember it before the war. It has regained its health, its fullness. Only my eyes remain hurt, distrustful, questioning.

We are in the vortex of one of the greatest migrations in history. As in the aftermath of a great storm, survivors of this colossal catastrophe are cast ashore, still in shock, trying to start a new life. Everyone's first problems are where to get clothes, shelter, and food. Once these necessities are met, every survivor asks the same questions: "Where is my family? I've survived, but who of my family is still alive, and how will I find them?"

Just a few weeks earlier, Europe was covered with a network of labor camps and concentration camps. At the whim of an SS man, family members were shot or separated by a thousand kilometers. Now, without regular railroad transportation, it is extremely difficult to get around or even to obtain information. Chaos reigns everywhere.

None of the means of modern technology is available for tracing and searching services. Survivors, still weak and often sick, can only wait and hope that conditions will improve.

I continue to occupy my small room in the German Museum. After work, I go to the coffee shop which has been organized in one of the large, undamaged halls and observe, fascinated, the hundreds of people who pass through. One can hear people from many countries speaking different languages. At night, a jazz orchestra plays old hits, tangos and foxtrots, reminders of prewar times. As I watch couples swaying and turning to the music, I remember dancing with Lydia in Warsaw, how we held one another close. Sometimes, when the memories are too painful, I go back to my room to be alone.

One night Dr. Ordecki and I are drinking watery beer in the museum coffeehouse. The orchestra is playing, and a young musician is clacking his maracas, singing *La Cucaracha*. Young couples are dancing, intoxicated with the rhythm. "It is incomprehensible," comments Dr. Ordecki. "Where do they get all this energy after years in the camps?" I have learned that he is addicted to morphine. Like many physicians with ready access to drugs, he uses it to dull his misery.

Near our table, a pretty young Gypsy woman raises her arms and swings her hips in time with the rhythm of the song. She is wearing an off-the-shoulder blouse. Large rings in each ear jingle as she dances. Her white teeth shine as she laughs. On her arm is a tattooed number from Auschwitz. "Beautiful woman," remarks Dr. Ordecki. "What a pity that Hitler destroyed so many of her people."

"It is a great pity," I reply. "The Gypsies died so quickly in the camps. They would trade their last piece of bread for a cigarette. Of a transport of a hundred who arrived at our camp, only a few survived."

"Hey, look at this couple," Ordecki interrupts, nodding towards a strapping American sergeant and a robust Russian girl. He moves with surprising grace and speed for such a large man and is trying to teach her the jitterbug. She imitates his movements, rather awkwardly, and laughs with uninhibited pleasure. Although they can hardly communicate, they are thoroughly enjoying each other's company. "A symbol of allied nations," observes Doctor Ordecki.

"Too bad they cannot find a common language," I remark. "The world's future depends on it."

The American notices that I am watching him. When the dance is over, he winks at me. "Hey you, come over here!" I approach his table. "Listen," he says, slightly drunk, "can you get me a bottle schnapps? I'll give you a carton of cigarettes."

"I'm sorry, Sergeant. I don't know where to get one."

"What? No schnapps? I must have some. And listen. I'm not a sergeant. I'm a general."

"Okay, General," I play along.

"She's a doll, ain't she? I need that schnapps real bad," he says, slipping his hand around the girl's waist.

I return to our table, where two young Poles have joined us. They argue about whether or not to return to Poland. "We Poles," one says, "were the first to try to stop Hitler. We spilled our blood from the beginning to the end on the battlefields of two continents. Many of us died in the camps. And now we ask ourselves the big question, shall we return home or shall we continue to wander? I dreamt of returning to a free Poland, but that cannot be. I intend to go to Italy and join General Anders' army of Polish volunteers."

"I will return to Poland," states his companion. "We must face reality, not live in a dreamland. There is so much we can do for our country."

As I listen to this conversation, I think of the tortured history of my native land, a country of courageous romantics, squeezed between two powerful neighbors. For the Polish Jews, though, Poland is only a graveyard. Not even a graveyard. The ashes of our families and friends have been dispersed by the wind, carried with the smoke from the chimneys of the crematoria. The Germans could count on the Poles' passive indifference, and even approval, of the massacre of the Jews. There were a few righteous Poles who risked their own lives to save Jews, but they were isolated individuals. Oppressed and enslaved themselves by the Germans, few of them had room in their hearts for the Jews who were killed in front of their eyes.

Three soldiers of the Jewish Brigade pass near our table. They wear British uniforms with white belts, and a band with David's shield on their arms. "*Shalom*, peace," they greet us.

Suddenly one of the Poles exclaims, "I cannot believe my eyes." He is visibly shaken. "Do you see that man in the grey suit dancing with the red-haired girl?"

"The man with the scar on his cheek?"

"Yes, him," he continues, very agitated. "He was a *Rapportführer* in Auschwitz. An Estonian in the service of the SS."

"Are you certain?"

"Yes, absolutely. It's unbelievable that he would come here. He must think that Munich is far enough from Auschwitz that no one would recognize him in civilian clothes."

"If you are certain, we cannot let him escape. Go to the entrance of the hall," I tell him, "and wait there. Don't let him leave." I hurry to the table where the sergeant and the Russian girl are whispering to each other.

"General, I need your assistance. I work for the American Military Government. Here's my identification. A Nazi criminal is in this room. Please go to the military station on Rosenheimerstrasse and come back with a jeep. Wait in front of the building and we'll bring the Nazi there."

The Sergeant becomes all business. He gives the Russian girl a pat on her backside, winks at her, and leaves quickly.

I approach the Estonian. "Come with me. Don't try to escape. It would be useless." He looks at my uniform and does not resist. Searching him in the next room I find, to my amazement, documents confirming that he was a *Rapportführer* in Auschwitz. The Pole and I take him to the street where, a few minutes later, the Sergeant and an MP pick us up in a jeep.

Returning to the German Museum later that night, I think about what I have done. The idea of seeking any kind of justice was impossible in the camps. To mete out justice myself then would have been unthinkable. I finally realize, now, that I am truly free.

Denazification

AT WORK, I sit in my office, reading hundreds of questionnaires, preparing summary after summary while the summer sun shines outside my window. I want to be outside, too, to have less paperwork and more contact with people. I ask Colonel Quirk for a more active job.

"Okay, young man. Find a car and you can become our first investigator."

One of the clerks in our office tells me that he knows of a six-cylinder Fiat which had belonged to the Wehrmacht Sanitary Park, now located some fifty miles from Munich. A few days later I manage to buy it from the US Military Government at a very low price and arrange for payments to be deducted from my salary in weekly installments.

My new job as an investigator involves observing different aspects of life in Germany and reporting on problems I detect. I interview hundreds of people from all walks of life, from the Prime Minister of Bavaria and his cabinet members to the people on the street. I try not only to analyze current affairs but also to detect new trends.

What I observe is that of the three objectives of the U.S. Military Government in Germany — demilitarization, denazification, and the implantation of the seeds of democracy — only the first is succeeding. It would be naive to believe in the pompous words of politicians which are quoted daily in the newspapers, claiming that the attitudes of Germans have miraculously changed, only a few months after the war. Years of indoctrination and the intoxication with having been the masters of Europe do not simply vanish after defeat. Denazification cannot be carried out like the amputation of an infected arm. The Nazi spirit is still very much alive. As to the ideals of democracy, they simply do not interest the Germans. There is no heroism or pathos in democracy. No cannons, no uniforms or parades. How does it compare to the euphoria of victories and conquests, to the elation of feeling superior? Is it not the fate of other nations to be subservient to Germany? Some politicians champion democracy, but most of the German people remain indifferent. To them, democracy means weakness.

The country is in a state of apathy and self-pity. There are few manifestations of repentance. A cabinet member tells me that former Nazi party members are merely "victims of the system." Many believe that Hitler's fault was not that he started the war, but that he was defeated. I often hear people say, "*Im Grunde Hitler war doch recht.* Hitler was basically right."

The Germans were afraid of the Allied victors and are surprised by their leniency, which they perceive as weakness. After a few months, their respect has changed to a flippant attitude with a hint of contempt toward the victors.

The main concern is the everyday economy. Following the defeat, the German standard of living has sunk. Yet, in spite of widespread destruction by Allied bombs, the conditions are still better than in most of the neighboring countries. Germans wear nice clothes, in striking contrast to the poor dress of the Poles, for example. But people in the neighboring countries, having been plundered for years by the Germans, are now more used to life's hardships. Bavarians complain bitterly about food shortages, although there is no real hunger. The fertile soil produces enough to eat, and most of the urban population have many possessions to barter for food. People have to adjust to some temporary deprivations, but their situation cannot be compared to the real hunger in countries that, not long before, suffered under the German boot.

Speculation and barter are widespread. The only currency to be trusted is the American dollar. American cigarettes and coffee are used as substitutes for the Deutschmark and, for bigger transactions, cameras and jewelry are used. All this creates the phenomenon of the *"Tauschgeschaefte,"* with goods being traded for other goods. Long columns offering barter exchanges are advertised in newspapers or on posters plastered on walls in the streets. Dishonesty and corruption pervade the economy. The guiding principle is, "If I don't cheat you, you'll cheat me." Most people are engaged directly or indirectly in black market activities. The crippled wheels of production have come almost to a standstill. Munich, a vibrant center of art and literature before Hitler, has become a cultural desert.

Young Germans are passive and cynical. They live in a vacuum, still susceptible to ideas based on old German values. Many *Fräuleins* aspire to catch American GIs. Sharp antagonism develops between the Bavarians and the German refugees, particularly those from the East. "They came to disturb our tranquility," Bavarians tell me. Years of terror, brutality, killing and pillage are followed by a German subservience that masks thinly veiled arrogance. Denial of guilt goes along with the claim that the German people were unaware of the atrocities committed for over six years.

One day, Herr Raff reads me a poem he has written. It is a funny, but frank account of the deception and denial we encounter every day among the Germans we interview:

> Now, *Herr Regierungsrat,* don't be a smarty.
> We have proof you joined the Nazi Party.
> It is stated right here that in '33,
> You joined the party with glee.
>
> But dear Sir, I implore you.
> It's all a mistake, I assure you.
> I helped the Jews whenever I could.
> It's not my fault, if away they were put.
>
> Please, Sir, I would have been fired.
> The *Gauleiter* ordered everyone retired
> If they objected to joining summarily,
> So I was forced to sign temporarily.
>
> So you did join, *Herr Regierungsrat.*
> Why didn't you say so at the start?
> You Nazis sure are all the same,
> Lying and arrogant without any shame.

"Herr Raff, you are one of the few Germans I've met who speaks or writes with such candor."

"That's probably because I lived in the States for many years. I had the bad luck to return to Germany just before the war broke out. And now I am truly afraid that Germany will never change."

"Why do you say that?" I ask.

"We were cruel in victory and servile in defeat. The Americans want to teach us democracy, but our generation is lost for democracy. America, England and France are countries of individualists. Germany is not. We are happy when somebody thinks for us so we can simply follow orders. That's why we are such good soldiers when it comes to discipline. The military conspiracy of 1944 and the students' plot in Munich were the only independent actions of any significance organized by Germans against the Nazis. Underground movements did not develop here. We know how to die as soldiers, but not how to be revolutionaries.

"Most of us consciously or unconsciously admire military strength. As children, we learned the gloomy *Nibelungenlied*. Kriemhild's vengeance was ingrained as a symbol in our young minds. Compare the bright beauty of the Greek mythology with the depressing Walhalla of our pathetic warriors. We read Nietzsche and learned to despise mercy, to value the Teutonic strongman. These values have not changed through the ages. Frederick the Great, Bismarck, Kaiser, Hitler, all of them understood the aspirations of our nation and followed the same ideals."

Herr Raff sighs. "The Americans should concentrate their efforts on re-educating our youth. Our only hope lies there."

Several other DPs join our staff in adjacent offices. I become good friends with another camp survivor, an exuberant young man about my age from Kovno, Lithuania. Frock talks constantly about his missing wife, exclaiming in Russian, "*Otdaytye mnye moyu Sonyechku!* Give me back my dear Sonya!" Because he is employed by the transportation department, he is able to acquire a small Ford convertible. We decide to make limited forays outside Munich on our days off, hoping to find some miraculous word of our wives.

The Autobahn traffic is thick with jeeps, trucks, and sedans driven by American officers. Only a few German private cars are allowed to circulate. At the entrance ramps to the Autobahn, crowds of Germans stand with outstretched arms, trying to hitch a ride. Frock drives by them, standing up and steering with one hand. With the other, he waves and shouts, "*Kaputt, Deutschland, kaputt!*" Once past, he drops back down into his seat, laughing merrily.

Our staff grows every day. Already seventy people work here. One day a handsome young American officer arrives to work in the office. Major Ordway is suave, cheerful and approachable. It is impossible not to like him. At first, he performs the same work as everyone else, and we never guess that he is to be our boss. He impresses me greatly. I feel that he likes me, too, partly because he knows that he can trust me more than the insincere German employees and, perhaps, because I am his first contact with a camp survivor.

Soon after his arrival, the major comes to see me. He hands me several shirts, a grey tweed suit, a blue overcoat and a pair of shoes, insisting that I try them on right there. They fit perfectly. I fall in love with the blue overcoat made of fine wool. I am overwhelmed with gratitude.

"I find no words to thank you, Major."

"Well," he smiles, "if you really want to thank me, I've got a job for you. My hobby is photography; I picked up a German manual about Leica cameras. Would you translate it for me after office hours? It will be a big job, I warn you."

"I'll be glad to, Major."

"Wonderful. But why are you smiling?"

"When the Russians first came to the West, Major, their passion was watches. They were all looking for *chassiki*. Now the Americans all want cameras, especially Leicas."

"It's true," the major agrees. "The Germans are leaders in optics and chemicals. We have a lot to learn from them in these fields."

I work diligently for several nights translating the manual. I am interested in photography myself and am very happy to do something for the major. When the translation is finished, I write on the front page, "To Major Ordway, my liberator, from a survivor of the concentration camps."

The same day, the major asks me to come to his office. Waiting for him, I notice two photographs on the wall. One is of General Patton, with a personal dedication. The other is a wedding picture of the major and his bride leaving a church under a canopy of crossed sabers held up by army officers. I turn away and remember Lydia on our own wedding day.

Lydia's face is radiant in the candlelight, her eyes full of love. The rabbi blesses us, and we seal our marriage with a kiss.

Has it been only six years? It seems a lifetime ago.

The major walks into the room with the customary bounce in his step, taking me out of my thoughts. He tells me he is happy with the translation, and very moved by the inscription. We spend some time together discussing the advantages and flaws of the Leicas. Finally, he puts down the manual and says, "I really appreciate your work in the office and the work you've done for me. You are a good investigator. Now tell me what I can do for you."

This is the moment I have prayed for. I choose my words carefully. "You've done a lot for me already, Major, but there is one thing that means more than anything else. I must find my wife. Until now, I've been too weak to do anything, but it's five weeks since I left Dachau, and I must start searching. I want to look in all the camps in Germany until I find her, or find someone who can tell me where else to look. Please, Major, don't refuse me this one thing. Please help me." It seems unlikely that he will agree to send me off on my own in return for a translation job, but I have nothing to lose by asking.

Major Ordway looks at me a long moment, then stands up and firmly shakes my hand. "Yes, Henry, of course. I can, and I will. I'll begin by giving you a pass to make it easy for you to travel throughout the American, French and British zones in Germany. How does that suit you?"

That night I cannot sleep. I am back in Warsaw with Lydia and our families, at the onset of the war.

Flight

NOVEMBER 12, 1939. Lydia and I are getting married by candlelight as bombs fall on Warsaw. We are all huddled together in Lydia's parents' apartment. Our parents are all there; my brother, Maurice; my twin sister, Edwarda; Szymon, my sister's husband; and the Rabbi. It is dark outside, and the streets are filled with rubble. It is dark inside too, except for the flickering candlelight. Luckily, the apartment is only partly damaged. Water still drips from the faucets. Because of the danger, our wedding is reduced to only the basic ceremony, without a Huppah and all the traditional Jewish rituals.

It is a solemn scene. Lydia's father, thoughtful, tall and handsome, stands proudly next to his wife. The Rabbi hurriedly intones the prayers. Lydia's mother holds her husband's arm and cries quietly during the brief ceremony. Lydia takes after her mother, who is fair-complected and beautiful. My parents, a little older and greyer, also watch proudly, with moist eyes.

"Mazel-tov," my brother exclaims softly after the ceremony, and everyone embraces us. I turn to my new bride. She looks lovely, her warm hazel eyes smiling up at me, her light brown hair falling softly in waves. We kiss.

After the wedding, we have a painful, emotional discussion about what we should do. Lydia and I beg our parents to escape Warsaw with us, but they do not want to leave. The trip, they insist, would be too strenuous and risky at their age. "It's you young people who must escape," Lydia's mother says. "We will survive here somehow." My father agrees.

Finally, a decision is made that Lydia and I, Edwarda, Szymon and their seven-year old daughter, Misia, will try to reach the Russian-occupied part of Poland. Our parents will stay in Warsaw. My brother Maurice will stay, too, to give moral support to our parents, and protection, if need be. If we reach the Russian zone, out of the Germans' reach, I will return to organize the escape of our parents and Maurice.

Early the next morning, I walk along the ruined streets of Warsaw to the apartment of my friend, Ignas. I tell him of our plan and, right away, he decides to join us. Ignas knows someone who owns a horse and an old wagon in a stable close to his home. We find the owner and, after some haggling, buy the horse, the wagon, and a supply of hay. We return to Lydia's parents and prepare to leave.

We wait until the last possible moment. Lydia's mother kisses her, her only child. We embrace one another as we say good-bye to our parents and Maurice. Ignas takes the reins. Looking back, we wave good-bye, trying to hold back the tears.

Outside Warsaw, we have some good luck and manage to by-pass several German guard posts. We cross the Bug River, reach the Russian-occupied territory of Poland, and find ourselves in Lida, a small town south of Vilno, about ten miles from the Lithuanian border. Ignas separates from us in Lida to find his own way across the border.

We find a guide to lead us across the border. Pan Jozef is a tall, muscular man who sports a long Polish-style mustache that he likes to twist between his thumb and index finger. He is familiar with the countryside around Lida and knows every out-of-the-way path and hideaway on the stretch to Eyshishke, a hamlet in Lithuania a few miles north of the border. We make a deal that he will lead us across the border, sealing it with a handshake. Pan Jozef receives one-third of his fee in advance, the balance to be handed over after we reach Eyshishke.

Every night we watch the moon, hoping that it will disappear behind the mist and clouds, but there are no clouds. Night after night the moon looks down at us with a cartoon-like, mocking grimace. We wait impatiently. With obscured visibility, we will have a better chance of sneaking unnoticed across the border from the Russian-occupied part of Poland to Lithuania which is still quasi-independent. We hope that once in Lithuania, some miraculous gate will open for our escape from the seething turmoil of Europe.

"We cannot wait any longer," Pan Jozef finally decides. "There are rumors that in a day or two the Russians will double the number of guards. Too many refugees have tried to cross the border, and some have been caught. The border patrols are on the alert. Moonlight or not, we must try tonight."

At nightfall, we walk the cobbled streets of Lida, past the poor one-story houses, until we reach the open countryside. We make our way between snow-covered groves and bushes. A few times Pan Jozef tells us to lie down so as not to be seen and, after a while, we continue on our way.

The moon and the stars cast a silvery-blue light that makes the landscape around us look like an enchanted dreamland. Icicles glitter on the branches of the trees, throwing sparkles of light on the snow. It is very cold. Lydia, like the others, valiantly moves forward with a rucksack on her back. Little Misia falls asleep. Usually lively and outgoing, she looks so innocent now, in repose. My sister carries Misia on her back. Edwarda isn't strong, but she does not complain, even though Misia must be heavy. Szymon carries his rucksack as well as my sister's. He stops every so often to wipe the sweat off his horn-rimmed glasses.

My rucksack is the heaviest of all. In it are two long loaves of black peasant bread. Before we left, I dug large holes in the bread and inserted rolls of gold coins in each, large American "Eagles" and smaller French "Napoleons." I filled the cavities in the loaves with kneaded bread to conceal the holes. I am carrying a fortune.

We walk through a grove facing a field of some hundred yards. Pan Jozef directs us to lie down and scans the horizon to detect any danger. Finally, he tells us to run as fast as we can to reach another grove at the end of the plain. We run in a line one after another. Faster! Faster! We are almost there. So far so good. Just a few more steps.

"Koodah, Pastoy! *Halt!*"

I look back. A soldier has materialized out of nowhere. He is wearing a spiked Mongolian-style wool helmet — a Russian. He is several yards behind me.

Adrenaline pumps through my body; my heart throbs. I think: If they find the gold, we'll be in great trouble. Who knows what they will do to "capitalists"?

I stop next to a bush. Slowly, I push down the shoulder straps of my rucksack and, trying to conceal my movements, throw it into the snow next to a bush. I walk a few steps toward the group. Two other soldiers emerge from nowhere.

One of them must have noticed my maneuver. He picks up the rucksack from the snow.

We are ordered to march to a truck, which takes us to a military guardhouse. In front of a low wooden building, Lydia and I are separated from Edwarda, Szymon, and little Misia, who is now fully awake and looking around with curiosity. Lydia is ordered to wait in an anteroom, and I am led into another room to be interrogated by a Russian officer.

"So we have caught a capitalist," he says, smiling. He has a broad face and mustache, like Stalin's. He continues to smile, as he plays with the stacks of gold coins from my rucksack piled on his desk, rearranging them. Then he looks up at me, still smiling. "We can use men like you for hard labor."

I feel tired, drained of energy. "Oh, God," I sigh.

Suddenly there is no smile. He is angry, red-faced. "Your God, damn him, will not help you now. You'll start a new career in prison."

After the interrogation, Lydia and I are led out of the guardhouse and ordered to get into the back of a truck. One soldier takes the driver's seat, and another guards us in the back.

The truck reaches a highway just as the dawn begins to break. There is very little traffic. Once in a while we pass a peasant atop a horse-drawn cart with a load of hay or vegetables. Then the silhouettes of two men appear walking on the side of the highway toward us. Our truck stops, and one of the soldiers orders the men to get in.

"Yurek!" Lydia exclaims when she recognizes our friend from Warsaw. He is with his cousin.

The soldier forbids us to talk. We sit facing one another, amazed, hardly able to refrain. What irony, I think. How often the three of us have enjoyed each other's company.

Yurek has a wonderful sense of humor, and his profession as a commercial artist gives him a certain distinction. He is tall, broad-shouldered, and strikingly handsome. His features seem to have been carved by a master sculptor's chisel. Just a few months earlier, we vacationed together in Druskieniki, a summer resort on the Niemen River. The large restaurant of the hotel was always full in the morning. I had been amused by the coquettish glances the girls gave Yurek every time he entered the dining room.

And now we can only look at each other.

Huts, barns, and small houses appear alongside the road again as we enter Lida. The truck stops. We are ordered to enter a two-story stucco building. Yurek and his companion are separated from us on the main floor. We are led down to the basement through a corridor that connects two rooms. Lydia is taken to the smaller room, where I notice three other women. I am ordered to the larger room, where there are about twenty prisoners sitting on the floor or lying on beds of board.

As I lie staring at the wall, I think about how unexpected the whole chain of events has been, what an abrupt departure from my normal life. It doesn't seem that I am the one experiencing all of this. I feel more like a detached spectator watching the events as they play out before my eyes like a film.

In the days that follow, I have long talks with the other prisoners. We are not treated badly. The morning and evening rations of kasha are filling. Sometimes we pass the time playing games. Our favorite is called "dupnik." One man kneels and the rest take turns vigorously slapping his backside. He has to guess who slapped him. If he guesses correctly, he is replaced by the one he identifies, who then kneels down to be slapped. It is a stupid, rough game, but it makes the time pass, and everybody seems to enjoy it. At first, I do not slap hard, not wanting to hurt anyone. But that makes it easy to guess who I am, which means I receive too many hits myself. I learn to hit harder.

Interrogations take place once or twice a week. Because Stalin is an insomniac, he often calls his high-ranking officers very late at night. They, in turn, call their subordinates to delegate Stalin's orders, and so on along the chain of command. Thus, from the top to the bottom of the hierarchy, all Soviet bureaucrats have had to change their lifestyle to be available at night. My interrogator is low on this chain of command. Often in the middle of the night, I am called up from the basement to be questioned.

From time to time some prisoners are taken away and others brought in. One afternoon, a new prisoner enters our cell. He stands for a while in the door and looks around at our faces. His demeanor gives him an air of dignity and distinction. He chooses a place on the plank beside me. "I am Wawelberg," he introduces himself. This is one of the most distinguished Jewish names of Warsaw. He is a millionaire, known and respected for his generous philanthropy. We soon become friends. The games of dupnik *stop. Somehow, we are embarrassed to play in front of him.*

The prisoners in the cell are always curious about the interrogations and often talk about them. After a few days we begin to suspect a "rat" among us and talk only when he dozes off. One night, when the rat has fallen asleep and when we can hear him snoring, Wawelberg whispers to me about how he and his wife tried to cross the border. They were caught and brought to this prison because of their invaluable jewels. The interrogating officer jeered at them as he said: "Twice did Russia enrich its treasury. Once with the Tsarina's jewels, and the second time with Wawelberg's."

I am amazed the next day when Wawelberg tells me that the questioning officer at his interrogation knew almost every word of our conversation. The "rat" turns out to be smarter than us.

One night, a Russian officer says to me, "Your wife was interrogated last night, and revealed that she is pregnant. We have no facilities here for such a situation, so we have decided to let you go. You will both leave tomorrow."

That night I cannot sleep. Could Lydia be pregnant with our first child? Normally, nothing would delight me more. But how can we bring a child into the world under these circumstances? What will we do?

The next morning Lydia and I are allowed to leave the prison.

"Are you pregnant?" I ask as soon as we are out of hearing range.

"No, Henyu," she says, laughing. "I didn't really think that the trick would work. But they believed me! I just stuffed my clothes with padding — a bit more each time."

What an extraordinary woman I've married, I think, feeling both relief and disappointment. I want to have children, but not now.

My beard has grown in prison, so the first thing I do is go to a barber. Lydia waits while my beard is shaved and my long hair cut. Then we walk to the outskirts of town to Pan Jozef's house. He and his wife receive us warmly and tell us that Edwarda, Szymon and Misia are waiting in Lithuania. "You will rest here tonight," Pan Jozef says, "and we will try again tomorrow."

The following night, Lydia and I, with our rucksacks on our backs, follow Pan Jozef again to the outskirts of the town. On this night, clouds are covering the moon and stars.

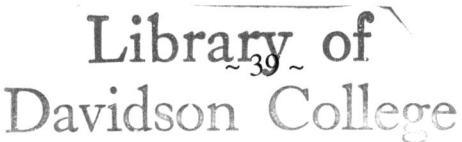

We cannot see further than a few steps, but Pan Jozef knows the way well, and we hike without fear of being spotted.

We trudge through knee-deep snow. After a few hours, Lydia gets tired. I take her rucksack, but she slows down anyway. We stop for a while to rest in a narrow ravine, then continue on. I try to encourage Lydia by saying now and again: "It's not far now, another kilometer or two." She, in turn, reminds me over and over to move my fingers so they don't get frostbite.

Flakes of snow fall softly upon us. They caress our faces and melt on our eyes. All is silent. Drabness and greyness disappear, and the world is wrapped in pure, chaste white. I think: Human beings resemble snowflakes in their endless diversity. Not one man or woman is like any other. And like snowflakes, we exist only a fleeting moment, suspended on a precipice between the incomprehensible past and the unfathomable future.

I have plenty of time to think. There are many kilometers to walk, and it seems that our trudging will never end. But the moment comes when Pan Jozef turns to us and announces with a smile: "We are in Lithuania."

It is dawn. Pan Jozef knows of an address in Eyshishke, the house of a Jewish family. Almost every night, he tells us, refugees who have crossed the border come to this place. When we arrive, the family receives us with much hospitality, and we all enjoy a good breakfast. We pay Pan Jozef with some jewels that Lydia managed to hide and bid him a safe journey back to Lida. Our host drives us in a one-horse wagon to the railroad station. After a couple of hours on the train, we arrive in Vilno, where we are reunited with Edwarda, Szymon, and little Misia. They tell us that the Russians permitted them to cross the border, probably taking pity on the child.

We also find Yurek in Vilno. He and his cousin were released after a short interrogation. The same night they tried to cross the border. It was extremely cold. Yurek made it unscathed, but his cousin's toes were frozen and became infected. Without anything to stop the infection, it spread rapidly through his body. They reached Vilno, but after a few days, Yurek's cousin died.

The Search

"**I**'M DRIVING, I'm driving, I'm driving a Fiat Six." I sing my song as I press down on the accelerator. The speedometer reads 95 kilometers per hour. I notice two silhouettes ahead of me on the Autobahn. It must be a check point, I think, as I push down on the brake. Two American military policemen approach my car, one very tall and the other short.

"Your pass."

"Here it is." The short one reads it aloud, word for word, slowly. I don't think he reads very well. "Pass to travel within U.S. zone by car en route to Bremen via Hamburg, Hanover, and Darmstadt to visit Displaced Persons camps. Facilities of the Military Government and UNRRA will be made available for housing, meals and gasoline. Request is made to British and French officials for similar cooperation."

"Okay," he says, relieved to have gotten through it. "It looks all right to me. Drive on."

I look at a sign at the side of the road: "To Augsburg — 30 kilometers." I pull a small, red velvet box out of my pocket and snap it open to reveal a gold wedding ring. I bought it recently from Olek, a survivor I knew from the Dautmergen concentration camp. He always knew how to barter, and somehow he has managed to become a small-time jewelry merchant in Munich's black market. "If I find Lydia," I told him, "I will give her this ring." I hope that I will be able to place it on her finger soon.

I pass through Augsburg, then Ulm, the birthplace of Einstein, and reach Stuttgart at midday. In the office of the French military authority, I find a list of former labor camps in the French Occupied Zone. I drive on to Heidelberg, where I find a private room for the night. The next morning, I continue driving through Mannheim-Ludwigshafen and reach Frankfurt in the evening. I spend the night in a very old Gothic church overlooking the Main River. Some priests have arranged a refuge there for transient lodgers.

On the third day, I approach Hildesheim to look in an abandoned labor camp nearby. I am alone in the midst of large blocks of concrete, barbed wire and rubble. No one in the town can tell me anything. Whenever I recognize former camp inmates by their clothes and general appearance, I stop the car and ask if by chance they knew Lydia. No one does.

I spend a few days at Bergen-Belsen, talking with many survivors of this massive concentration camp. I was very nearly sent here at one point. They know nothing of Lydia, but my inquiry opens the floodgates of their own loss. Where are their wives, their husbands, their sisters, brothers, parents, children? It is almost unbearable to listen to them, to see the despair in their eyes. I have come begging for answers, and I am met only with the agonized questions of others.

I am struck by the pitiful existence of these former inmates, trapped in the same barracks in which they were imprisoned, now referred to as DP camps. So many people still live in these camps. In Bergen-Belsen alone, there are still some twenty thousand. Life in the DP camps is similar in many respects to life under the German yoke; the same dull, grey, wooden barrack, the same lines to the kitchen for food. The former inmates are bewildered by freedom and wait for some action from the outside. They have survived by a miracle or, rather, by a series of miracles. Ten people are dead for every one who survived. The survivors still do not control their lives. What else can they do but wait?

As I continue to Bremen and Hamburg, the panorama of postwar Germany passes before my eyes. The Autobahn, the only positive work left by Hitler, is full of traffic. Jeeps, trucks and convoys rush by. People trudge by on both sides of the road: German prisoners of war returning from the East in threadbare Wehrmacht uniforms, civilians dragging small wooden carts loaded with their belongings, foreigners, survivors of concentration camps and labor camps. I continue, stopping to ask passers-by who look like former camp inmates, "What city are you from? In which camps have you been? Do you know anything about the camps for women?"

As I leave the Autobahn, I drive through towns in ruins, skeletons of houses, and more piles of concrete blocks. Turning to rural highways, I pass through idyllic, untouched hamlets and villages. Some are within a few miles of concentration camps. I wonder what the small-town Germans thought as they went about their daily lives, milking their cows, greeting one another, all in the shadow of such horror. Did it bother them? Could they simply ignore what was happening behind that barbed wire?

I drive by day and, when darkness approaches, I look for lodging for the night. On the tenth day, I arrive at the camp of Neustadt, near the border of Denmark. There I see a young woman I identify as Jewish by her melancholy eyes. As always, I ask her if she knows of a woman named

Eugenia Lydia Lilienheim. "She is twenty-six, very pretty," I say, seeing Lydia before my eyes, "with light brown hair and hazel eyes. We were married at the beginning of the war," I explain. "Her maiden name was Turkus."

"Yes, I know something of Lydia," the woman responds, and my heart begins to pound. I can hardly contain myself and beg her to tell me everything. All she knows is that in September, 1944, Lydia was sent from the labor camp Kaiserwald near Riga in Latvia, to the Stutthof camp near Gdansk, and later to the Polta ammunition factory in Magdeburg. I feel a mix of hope and despair. At last I have some news about Lydia, but I can't do anything with it. Magdeburg is in the Russian zone and my pass from the American Government does not provide access there.

I drive slowly. The car rattles and groans, echoing my thoughts. It is the fourteenth day of my journey and I am on my way back to Munich. I have asked hundreds of people, everybody whom I recognized as a former camp inmate, whether they knew anything about the camp in Magdeburg. Nobody could tell me anything. The car continues rattling. "It needs water," I tell myself and turn off the Autobahn. I take the first side road and come to a village inn.

Two young men sit on a wooden bench in front of the inn, drinking beer in the shade of an elm tree, two motorcycles parked nearby. Both men are around nineteen or twenty, one dark, the other fair. From their emaciated faces, short hair, and the guarded look in their eyes, I recognize them as former camp inmates. I sit down next to them.

"How enjoyable," I remark, "to drink cold beer on such a hot day. Where are you going, may I ask?"

"We're riding through Germany," the dark-haired man replies. "I'm trying to find my father. We were separated two years ago when I was sent to a labor camp. My friend, here, is looking for his sister who was in Auschwitz."

"What camp were you in?"

"The Polta ammunition factory, in Magdeburg."

"Magdeburg!" I can't believe it. "I've been looking everywhere for someone who was in Magdeburg. Did you know my wife, Eugenia Lydia Lilienheim?"

"No, I didn't know anyone of that name. But we were separated from the women and knew them only by sight. Do you have a picture of your wife?"

"No." I describe her, as I have done so many times.

They look uneasy. I try to read their thoughts from their faces. There is an uncomfortable silence.

"Why don't you tell me?" I finally exclaim. "I prefer the truth to uncertainty. Tell me everything."

After another moment of silence, the dark-haired one replies, "All right, I'll tell you. You've been in the camps yourself and you must be hardened to many things. Your wife may be alive, but it is also quite possible that she was killed. The Polta factory is near the Elbe River. When the Americans were coming from the West and the Russians from the East, the Germans drove us under heavy guard to the bank of the Elbe. In the confusion, we escaped. We hid in the ruins of a building and waited twenty-four hours until we saw the first liberators. We heard later that the camp inmates were taken to a place near the river and massacred. But some were able to get away. You must hope that your wife was among those who escaped."

I drive in a daze back to Munich and fall into my bed at the German Museum. My brow is covered with perspiration. I hear Lydia cry and try to cover my ears.

I run a fever for several days. Scenes from my childhood keep flashing through my mind.

"How difficult it is," my father says, "to find the right words to express feelings and thoughts." I see his noble face, his crown of white hair as he looks over a page he has just written. "Words are like musical notes. By themselves they have no life. They begin to live only when they are combined into chords and phrases, then into symphonies of glorious meaning. I hear such music in my head, but I cannot find the right words to put on the page. An impression haunts my mind, but when I try to describe it, the words escape me. That's why I read what I have written again and again, and try each time to find a better way to convey the original idea. A writer knows how remote his words are from the perfect music in his mind."

My father bends his head over the page and continues to write.

"Enough of your writing," my mother calls, hurrying into the room. "Shabbat supper will be ready soon, and the children will come any minute now."

Two silver candlesticks stand on the table, their candles burning brightly. My mother places her hands over the candles and closes her eyes. The light of the candles casts a golden glow on her face. She prays for the tranquillity of her home, for the health and happiness of her husband, her three children and granddaughter, for peace on earth and for blessing on all people of goodwill.

I wake up in a sweat, her prayer on my lips, and realize I was dreaming.

Did I know how much I loved her as I watched her pray that Friday evening? How much I loved my father? It was so natural to have parents, to be with them every day. I did not understand then how precious those moments were, and what my parents meant to me.

Hope

"YOU MUST REST for some time yet," Doctor Ordecki says. "Do not think about going back to work. It has been only two months since you were released from the camp, and you still have a long way to go before you regain your health. Try not to brood about the past. Perhaps your wife was among those who managed to escape. You have no proof that she is dead. Let us hope for the best. Now, rest quietly. I'll come back again this evening."

I lie prostrate in my bed in the German Museum, in the room overlooking the river. Dr. Ordecki attends to me with unusual care. A young Belgian, a new resident in the museum, brings my meals. The river roars beneath my window. Nothing else disturbs the silence of my room.

As I mull over and over the news about the massacre at the Elbe, I come to realize that there is a ray of hope. Lydia could possibly have escaped the massacre. I know that everyone else in my family was killed. But Lydia may still be alive.

As I begin to recover, I occasionally venture out to sit on a bench in the courtyard or at a table in the coffeehouse of the German Museum. I am working on a second translation for the major, about color photography. It diverts me somewhat, providing a contrast to my grey life. I meet many survivors. They are all desperately trying to find their loved ones. As information begins to trickle in, most of them learn how few members of their families are still alive. Survivors seldom find more than one relative, seldom learn the circumstances of their loved ones' death, or even the name of the camp where they died. Only in rare cases do a husband and wife find each other. The enormity of the Germans' crimes is becoming increasingly evident.

Railroad trains begin to run, bringing new waves of DPs to Munich, first from the entire American zone, then from the French and British zones. UNRRA organizes camps for the DPs. The first and largest Jewish camps near Munich are in Feldafing and Landsberg, each providing temporary shelter for about five thousand people.

Groups of DPs organize committees to represent themselves. A Jewish committee is set up in the German Museum, and plywood partitions are banged up to create office cubicles. The committee's most important task is to organize a search office. Pamphlets are printed under the Hebrew title, *"She'rit Hapletah*, The Remaining Survivors," with the names of survivors. Some Jews call themselves by this name rather than the impersonal "DP."

In the middle of July, 1945, the law of non-fraternization with Germans is abolished. In the evenings, streets and gardens swarm with couples. A love market springs up near the banks of the Isar River, close to the German Museum.

"Hey, *Fräulein,* do you want some chocolate and cigarettes?" ask buoyant young Americans. They prove irresistible to many of the German women, even among the aristocracy. Many of the young Americans are inexperienced in love affairs, but their boyish awkwardness appeals to the jaded women. German men watch while many of their wives and sweethearts prostitute themselves. Leaflets and graffiti appear in the streets:

> German women? After long weeks, we soldiers have come back, tired, on wounded feet, with only one question: "What will happen to the Fatherland?"
>
> We were prepared to meet the worst, but what we found cannot be expressed in words. German women are shamelessly whoring with foreigners. We can see them going off in twos and threes. We can see them in every doorway wearing impudent smiles on their faces.
>
> Aren't you ashamed, you German women? You know you are dragging us all in the dirt. The enemies needed six years to defeat the German soldiers. It takes only five minutes to capture a German woman.
>
> We have no cigarettes or butter to give you, no coffee or sugar. The foreigners offer you all this. And when they have chocolate, even the color of their skin does not matter.
>
> We wish you much pleasure, German women, and hope that the Russians will get you soon. Then you will receive your due, and no man will covet you anymore.

The last words refer to the Russian rape of German women during the first weeks of victory, and the alleged high rate of venereal disease among the soldiers. As the plague of VD spreads, German women claim they contract it from black GIs, while the Americans complain that they receive this gift, which they jokingly call the *"Veronika, dankeschoen,* Veronika, thanks a lot," from German women.

One afternoon, an extraordinary thing happens. I see three young women in the court of the German Museum and stop to talk. They have been friends since their childhood in Vilno, and they speak with sorrow of their lost families. It is obvious that they are camp survivors. I ask them whether they were in Magdeburg, and whether they knew my wife.

"Lydia. Oh, yes? Of course we knew her," they say in chorus. I cannot believe my ears. Finally, a breakthrough! The tall blond continues, "She was with us in Magdeburg. A very brave woman. She told me once that, if she survived, she would go back to Warsaw to look for you and her family. On the day of the evacuation, she escaped with another woman, just before we reached the shore of the Elbe River." She takes my hand and looks into my eyes. "You must know that if anyone could survive, it would be Lydia. She is such a strong, clever person. You must keep up your hope."

I go straight to Major Ordway and tell him what I have heard. He issues a pass in English, Russian and Polish that guarantees my passage, as well as Lydia's:

> This is to certify that the bearer is employed in the American Military Government and that he is proceeding through Czechoslovakia to Poland and to the Russian occupation area in Germany with the purpose of locating his wife, who was in a German concentration camp.
>
> It is requested that American, Russian, Polish and Czechoslovakian Military and Civilian Authorities assist Henry Lilienheim in his task and make such housing and mess facilities available, as well as radio, press and all other means which can help him to locate his wife. A further request is made to permit his wife to

cross the border with him on his return to the American occupation area for his work in the American Military Government.

I feel my hope renewed. I will not give up. I remind myself of all the times in the camps when I nearly gave up, only to fight my way back to life. Better to battle the dark forces than succumb to despair.

That night I dream about the miracle of our survival in the early days of the war.

Escape Plans

*M*Y FRIEND FEFERBERG *waits until everyone is asleep. Along with him and his wife, there are eight other people in the room, including Lydia, my sister Edwarda, little Misia, and myself. A few people are snoring and, once in a while, someone moans. Feferberg kneels besides the bed and pulls a suitcase out from under it. It is battered but sturdy.*

It has been months now since the Germans seized Vilno, driving out the Russians. We tried to escape, but it was too late.

Feferberg is a quiet man of about fifty, short, stocky, and bald. He has gentle, brown eyes. In Warsaw, he was a wealthy importer of watches. When he and his wife fled, he took a suitcase packed with his most expensive watches. He plans to bribe his way out of Europe and go to Venezuela, where he has relatives. When he heard that I knew Spanish, he engaged me as a tutor for himself and his wife.

I am not really asleep, and I watch Feferberg now. He unlocks his suitcase and lifts the lid. I see hundreds of gold and platinum watches inside. Some watches are framed with tiny, glittering diamonds. Feferberg takes a small linen bag from his pajama pocket and puts into it several bejewelled ladies' watches. It is enough wealth to bring him and his

~ 53 ~

wife, as well as Lydia, Edwarda, little Misia and me to a safer place. Szymon is no longer with us, and we are in mourning for him. He was taken away to a labor camp near a lake, where he drowned. What were the circumstances of his death, we do not know.

The plan is to bribe Fritz, the lieutenant in charge of the Rudnicka Street gate of the Vilno ghetto. Fritz will allow his comrade, Feldwebel Weber, to enter the ghetto in a truck, then leave with a cargo of twenty-five people. Weber will have a certificate signed by Fritz saying that a specified number of "special artisans" are to be transferred to the Warsaw ghetto for work useful to the German army.

We are uncertain about the plan. From what we've been able to ascertain, it seems that the situation is relatively quiet in the Warsaw ghetto. There is hunger there but, as far as we know, no so-called "aktions" in the streets. In the Vilno ghetto, there have already been three "aktions." Tens of thousands of men, women, and children were caught and evacuated. We have no idea where they were taken. The fortunate ones who had yellow labor cards were left alone. The others, often whole families, were hunted down like animals in the streets and homes and secret bunkers. The cries of children frequently revealed their hiding places to the SS. At least our lives will not be threatened in Warsaw, and we will be reunited with our families. The watches are our best insurance for getting out of the present misery. Once in the Warsaw ghetto, we will think of further means of escape.

Feferberg looks at the watches with a faint smile. He lowers the lid of the suitcase, locks it, and pushes it back under the bed. Tired, he lies down next to his sleeping wife. Someone snores loudly, but Feferberg is not annoyed. There is still hope. The gold watches will buy safety or, at least, *escape from danger. Feferberg closes his eyes and falls asleep.*

The next morning at 7 o'clock, as usual, groups of workers leave the ghetto to work as furriers, carpenters, tailors, shoemakers, or watchmakers in various German workshops and military organizations. Lydia and I are in a group assigned to the military hospital at Antokol, a suburb of Vilno. We march from the gate of the ghetto on Rudnicka Street through the streets of Vilno past Gedymin's hill. Lydia has difficulty in keeping up with the brisk pace, and from time to time calls to the leader of our group: "Mr. Reshanski, please slow down a little." Lydia and I have unusual jobs. She works in a medical laboratory. I work in the hospital office.

The hospital is the largest German military hospital on the eastern front, with more than a thousand workers attending to thousands of wounded Germans. When the Russians entered Vilno in 1939, they established a hospital on the vast estate of the Sapiehas, a family of prominent Polish aristocrats. In June of 1941, the Germans entered Vilno, occupied the Russian hospital and reorganized it as a German hospital. The chief is Dr. Boekamp, a colonel, from the German town of Fulda. He is a portly, middle-aged man with a kind face. He wields enormous power. He decides when the soldiers and officers are rehabilitated and ready to be sent home, or back to the front.

One morning Dr. Boekamp calls me to his office. In a friendly manner, he tells me of his interest in studying the medical histories that the Russians left behind in the hospital library. He has been told that I know German and Russian, and that I could prepare translations. From time to time I meet with Dr. Boekamp to report on my progress. He *turns out to be a decent man. On one occasion he takes a firm stand against the Gestapo in a case involving Catholic nuns accused of charitable work of which the Gestapo disapproved. Dr. Boekamp orders that I be provided with extra food rations from the hospital kitchen, but the order is usually disregarded by the German cooks.*

Some of the Jewish workers are able to generate a small amount of income from their work in the form of bottles of schnapps, cigarettes, or anything else that can be traded for food back in the ghetto. Shoemakers are rewarded for repairing officers' boots, and tailors are the biggest "earners."

I do not have any of these lucrative skills and wonder what I can do to earn some income. Since I like to draw and write verse, I finally decide to make albums that the German officers and nurses can keep as a souvenir of the hospital. On the first page, I draw a half-broken column entwined with ivy and flowers which stands in a secluded place on the hospital grounds. On the second page, in red and black medieval German script, I write several lines which I hope will pluck the sentimental German heartstrings:

> So sicher wie immer kommt wieder der Mai,
> Wird kommen der Tag wo der Krieg ist vorbei.
> Nach Jahren und Tagen man wird sich erinnern
> Der Zeiten des Sturmes, man wird sich entsinnen
> Der Städte und Plätze wo man damals war.
> Und hat man geschaut auf die folgenden Seiten,
> Kommt eine Erinnerung an die alten Zeiten.
>
> *As sure as May comes every year,*
> *The time will come when this storm is over.*
> *Years later you will think of the war*
> *And remember the places you once were.*
> *A look at the following pages*
> *Will remind you of these times.*

The album includes several more illustrations of fragments and facades of buildings, and a bird's eye view of the hospital grounds.

I work a few days on each album. Whenever I have the occasion to talk with a nurse or an officer, I show the album. "Ach, das ist ja wunderbar. Ich werd' dies ja meiner Mutti senden. *Ah, this is wonderful. I will send it to my mother," exclaims my first customer, a nurse. Most of my "clients" are eager to send their albums home to Germany. They don't care whether I drink from the bottle of schnapps they give me in return. I smuggle the schnapps into the ghetto to barter for a precious loaf of bread.*

One misty and chilly October evening, after our work at the hospital, Lydia and I walk, as usual, to the truck which waits to bring our group back to the ghetto. Lydia takes a seat next to the driver. The men climb into the rear of the truck. I am the last one. Just as I jump to get into the truck, it moves back toward the wall behind me. I am squeezed between the truck and the wall. My thighbone is crushed. I hear screams. The truck moves slightly forward, releasing me, and I fall into the truck. Lydia runs to the back and climbs in behind me. I feel nothing for awhile, but as we drive along the rough cobbled streets of Vilno, sharp pains begin to shoot through my leg, and I am shocked to find I can turn it in either direction.

The truck enters the ghetto, and I am rushed to the operating room of the hospital. An aged surgeon performs an operation to straighten and stabilize my broken leg. The operation is not successful. Lydia decides to take matters into her own hands. She makes up her mind that two outstanding doctors will perform a second operation. She decides first on Dr. Pejsachowicz, a surgeon at the ghetto hospital. Then she sets her sights on the unthinkable task of bringing Doctor Michejda, a specialist at Vilno University and a gentile, to the ghetto hospital.

The next morning, audacious as always, and disregarding all peril, Lydia removes her yellow star and ventures outside the ghetto. No one, thank God, stops her to check for her papers. She finds Doctor Michejda's residence, and somehow persuades him to undertake the dangerous risk of venturing into the ghetto to perform this humanitarian deed. Then she bribes the guard at the ghetto gate, and Doctor Michejda is let in.

Michejda and Pejsachowicz bore a hole below my knee and insert a metal rod. They attach the rod to a rope which is then wound over a counterweight suspended on the footboard of the bed. The purpose is to gradually straighten the broken parts of the bone until they can be aligned. And so begin the long, long months of lying flat on my back.

One of the patients in the hospital is a man named Salzberg. We met earlier, while Vilno was still under Russian occupation. He is a funny man who loves telling jokes. When the Russians began their evacuation of Vilno, many refugees, including Lydia and me, went into hiding until the transports were discontinued. Salzberg was so afraid of being sent to the interior of the Soviet Union that he slit his own throat in a fit of despair. The doctors managed to save him by performing a tracheotomy.

"Oh what I would give to be in the middle of the Soviet Union now," Salzberg says now in his hoarse, throaty voice, as he sits by my bed. I nod my head in agreement.

One day Feferberg, our prospective benefactor and key to our escape, comes to see me. "You know," he says sadly, "I was prepared to give whatever watches were necessary so that you and your family could escape with us to Warsaw. What a pity that you will have to stay in bed for sev-

eral months. We must leave in two days. I deeply regret that you cannot escape with us."

This is a bitter disappointment. Our lives would be so much safer in Warsaw, I believe, while in Vilno we are in constant danger.

Two weeks later, a nurse tells me the story of Feferberg's escape. The truck left the ghetto with twenty-five people. Instead of the three-hundred mile ride to Warsaw, they were driven a few miles to the Lukishki prison in Vilno, right into the clutches of the Gestapo. Lieutenant Fritz and Feldwebel Weber were informants. Feferberg, his wife and fellow prisoners were held for a short time and then shot.

Liquidation

IN THE SPRING OF '43, Lydia and I learn the tragic news of the Warsaw ghetto uprising. The remaining Jews have made a desperate, heroic last stand against the Nazis. Almost all of them have been killed, or sent to death camps. I know that my parents and my brother could not have survived.

How did they perish? Where are their bodies? What were their dying words?

I rage against their fate. I want to kill or be killed, but I am a caged animal who can do little more than bite the bars of my prison with his bare teeth. I imagine the burning houses of Warsaw. I see the streets, each holding a fragment of our lives. I see families in a sea of flames. Mothers clutching their children, knowing that in a moment they will die together. I see thousands of eyes, wide open, staring in horror, holding the last image they will see, the faces of their murderers. I see my mother. She calls my name. I hear her bless her husband and children with her last breath. What did these hearts feel in the face of death? What thoughts ran through their minds? Did you hear their voices, you silent God?

A few months later, on the 23rd of September, the Vilno ghetto is liquidated. After a desperate effort at resistance, several thousand of us are forced to leave for Estonia. We pass through a cordon of German SS and Ukrainian guards that extends for a mile from the gate of the ghetto to a dead end street called Rossa. The cordon bristles with machine guns.

I walk with Lydia, Edwarda, and little Misia.

"What a pity, Henryk," says my sister, "that you didn't escape to the forest with the others. Perhaps you, at least, would have survived." She is crying silently.

"I couldn't leave you, Eda. I did not want to save myself without all of you."

My sister holds Misia's hand. I look at the sweet face of my little niece, at her sad eyes that have seen too much. She smiles up at me, as if to reassure me. I feel such love and tenderness for her, such despair. My little Misia, I remember the day when you were born. I remember bending over your cradle. I remember how we played together, how you were singing and joking, and how you tried to console me when I lay in the hospital with a broken leg. Why are you punished? How much agony I feel for you. How much I love you.

"Eda," I say to my sister, "I do not know whether we are going to our death or not. May God protect you and Misia."

My sister and I are quiet. I cannot do anything. I would willingly give my life to save my wife, my sister and niece.

Lydia is restless. She does not want us to give up our lives so easily. She still wants to run, to try to escape, not to die without a fight. She looks for some opening, an empty place in the cordon of guns, any opportunity however risky. But there is no opening. Germans or Ukrainians stand guard on both sides.

"Are we going to our death?" Lydia asks one of the Ukrainians in Russian.

"Nyet, na rabotoo," he replies, laughing. *"No, to work."*

I tell Lydia, *"I was not as good a husband as I wanted to be. Forgive me. Tell me that you forgive me."*

She does not reply or even listen. She is looking around, still searching for a way for us to escape.

Suddenly I feel a blow on my back as I am roughly shoved to the right. I do not realize what has happened until I see Lydia, my sister and niece disappearing through a gate to the left.

"Men to the right, women to the left," I hear a German command. I find myself in the middle of a crowd of men. I feel completely indifferent about what will happen to me. I can think only of Lydia, Eda and Misia. I am overwhelmed with guilt and humiliation that I can do nothing to save them.

For another hour, groups of people from the ghetto continue to arrive — men to the right, women to the left. Night is falling. It starts to drizzle. We sit on the ground facing machine guns. A truck arrives. As it stops in front of us, we hear the music of the popular German song, "Rosamunde." The merry, hideous tune sounds grotesque amidst thousands of prisoners who do not know whether they will live another hour. A few more records are played on a gramophone. Then the music stops. Silence.

A faint light begins to shine on the horizon. It becomes brighter and brighter until the whole circle of pale red sun fills the sky. Perhaps the last sunrise of our lives, I think.

A senior SS officer, Weiss, accompanied by two aides, picks his way among the prisoners. He orders us to stand at attention. Weiss is wearing a leather overcoat and shiny boots. It is clear that he finds it distasteful to get mud on his shoes, to get too close to the Jews. On his cap, a skull and *cross-bones stare ominously at us. Weiss points with his immaculately gloved hand at one of the men. "Forwärts! Step forward!" barks an aide. The finger slithers in front of our faces. Wherever it points, the victim has to step forward and join a separate group.*

I feel the breath of death, and a bitter taste in my mouth. My tongue is a block of wood. Something strangles my throat. I try to expand my chest and broaden my shoulders. Weiss's finger approaches the place where I am standing. Nothing can help me now. Hunger and exhaustion must be written all over my face. He will surely notice. This is the end.

The finger points at me.

Should I shut my eyes? I am so tired. No, I will hold them open and look straight into his eyes. He will not see fear in them.

"Komm, komm," I hear, "Come, come." I see red, then black. My tongue is swollen and hard, my head jerks away, but I keep my eyes open and see that the finger is directed not at me, but at my neighbor.

When the "selection" is over, all those chosen for death are taken away. Then four gallows are erected against the red wall in front of us.

A voice on a loudspeaker announces: "Four people who tried to escape will be hanged in front of you. This is to teach you a lesson. The same will happen to anyone who does not follow orders."

A woman and three men are brought to the wall. "That's Chwojnik, the one with the paralyzed hand," I hear a voice near me.

Yes, it is Chwojnik, a noble man, one of the organizers of the resistance. With him are the heavy-set watchmaker Levin, who still wears his thick glasses, Pavel, the slim, sad-eyed teacher, and a young girl, Tsenia, perhaps twenty-two years old, Pavel's girlfriend.

The four climb the ladders and stand on an elevated platform with their backs to us. They turn their faces in our direction.

Chwojnik gently shakes his head. We can see that he wants to say farewell to us. It seems to me that I understand his mute speech: "I perish, and millions like me will perish. But our death will bring freedom. The day of liberation will come for some of you. Endure, and let those of you who survive remember us."

One of the German aides places a noose around the necks of each of the victims. The other prepares to pull the ladders from under their feet. Chwojnik's paralyzed hand is still shaking. There is no expression on Levin's face. The girl smiles. How young and fresh she looks. The aide knocks away the ladders.

In a few minutes the girl is dead. The rope from which Levin hangs breaks under the weight of his heavy body. He falls to the ground. His glasses shatter. Oh, God!, I think, am I going crazy? Weiss orders Levin to kneel with his face toward the wall. What is Levin thinking as he looks so quietly at the wall? I cannot bear to watch as he waits for death. Why doesn't anyone scream? Why don't I scream? God, do you see? Do you exist?

Weiss walks over to Levin and places a revolver at the back of his neck. A moment later a stream of blood reddens the stones on the ground.

What is there to do? Run to Weiss, bite his throat, push my fingers in his eyes? Facing me are machine guns. I see the sneering faces of the Ukrainian guards, the hateful, wooden faces of the Germans. I look up. The girl's body hangs quietly. Chwojnik's body shakes with convulsions. The noose was too loose and did not close tightly enough to kill him right away. His legs move in the air and his whole body quivers spasmodically. His face is contorted with pain.

Germans, I hate you! Those of you who murder us now, and all others who silently acquiesce in these murders. Be damned, and damn the country that nourishes you.

We are ordered to leave. I take a last look at the hanging bodies. Chwojnik's corpse is finally still.

After travelling five days, crammed together in cattle cars, we arrive at Vaivara, a labor camp in the marshes and forests of Estonia. There I meet a girl who came from a camp near Riga where she has seen Lydia. When the women were separated from the men in Vilno, she tells me, the young, healthy and childless were gathered in one group. Older women and those who refused to leave their children were sent to death, probably to Treblinka or Auschwitz. Lydia's group was sent to the Kaiserwald labor camp next to a rubber factory near Riga. Edwarda and Misia, I realize, must be dead.

The Ruins of Warsaw

I LEAVE MUNICH in the morning, accompanied by an officer the major has assigned to take me safely through the Czech border. We arrive at the railway station in Pilsen. There I board the train for Prague and am soon passing through the lush green plains of Czechoslovakia.

At the next station, four Russians enter the compartment. They are in high spirits. One starts to play an accordion and the others sing Russian songs. It is the first time in four years that I have seen Russian soldiers. One of them tries to kiss the train conductor, an apple-cheeked young Czech woman. He holds her around her waist with one arm and tickles her under the chin. She pushes him back, laughing. The Czechs in the compartment laugh, too. The atmosphere is friendly and playful.

The Russian soldiers look dishevelled. They wear long tunics girded with broad belts. Ringlets of hair escape from under their caps and fall on their foreheads. They do not have the smart, clean look of the American soldiers. But there is something in the Russians that I do not see in the Americans. These Russians are soldiers, through and through. I feel it in every word, in every movement. It is easy to visualize Americans in civilian clothes. They would be only too glad to put away their smart uniforms, a reminder of the uncomfortable days of war. The Russians, on the other hand, look comfortable and natural in their shabby uniforms, like soldiers accustomed to the hardships of war.

Russians have a talent for suffering. No nation or people, with the exception of the Jews, has endured so much suffering in its history — invasions from the East and the West, subjugation by the Mongols, the tyranny of the Tsars. Suffering and pain have entered the Russian bloodstream, making them resistant to the most difficult conditions of life. In the concentration camps, the Russians showed great ability to endure and adapt. Still, only a fraction of the Russian prisoners of war survived. While the strength of the American army lies in its technical superiority and genius for innovation and organization, the strength of the Russian Army lies in the quality of its soldiers.

Passing through Czechoslovakia, I am impressed by the relatively minor destruction compared with the ruins of other countries of Central Europe. The Czechs have started to rebuild their lives with energy and skill. Prague, one of the most beautiful cities in Europe, combines the charm of the Middle Ages and Baroque period with modernity. After the ruins of the German towns, I am enchanted by the beauty of the main street, Vaclavska Namesti.

I spend two days in Prague, inquiring about Lydia at various organizations, but I do not obtain any useful information.

Crossing the Polish border, I am struck at once by the atmosphere of chaos and instability. The war passed over Poland like a raging storm and completely changed the face of the country. Millions of people died and millions more were dispersed. The national borders have been altered significantly, pushed back in the East and extended in the West. But it isn't only the borders that have changed, but the psychology of the people. I am shocked by a cynicism that did not exist before the war. The general attitude seems to be that everything is frail, shaky, temporary. Walls rebuilt today will only fall in ruins tomorrow.

Here are two Slavic peoples, I think, the Czechs and the Poles. The Czechs are adapting themselves to the new situation, while chaos reigns in Poland. Courage and romanticism, these are Polish traits. This nation bore Chopin, Copernicus, Curie. Poles love liberty and have always been ready to make great sacrifices for it. But they lack realism, tolerance, sober political and economic thought. This is a nation of farmers and knights-errant, not of diplomats and businessmen. They fought valiantly throughout the war, with no traitor among them. Yet, even in their suffering, most of them remained prejudiced and intolerant. They were infected by the German poison, the hatred of Jews. Now they hate the Germans and the Russians. When will the waves of hatred in this beautiful country subside?

The train rolls slowly into Warsaw's Central Station. People rise and stretch, and pull their parcels down from the racks. My heart pounds. I have dreamed so often of this day. I haven't been in my home town in over six years. Today I will see houses and streets, many of which hold fragments of my life — the Saxon garden lined with the chestnut trees where I used to play as a child, the streets I walked to school, the corner where I kissed a girl for the first time. Every step will bring back the days of my youth in the city I love.

But where will I find the grave of my parents? Where will I embrace the earth and weep for them? I want to implore them to forgive me for the sin of surviving when they have perished. I want to tell them that the wound inside me will never heal.

I take my rucksack from the rack. In a few hours, I will know if Lydia is alive. She must have come to Warsaw. I might even see her this very day. We will tell each other everything about the seven hundred days of our separation.

Several dilapidated trucks are standing in front of the station. "Whoever is going to Praga, get in here," a driver calls. I have the address of a committee on Szeroka Street in Praga, a suburb on the right bank of the Vistula River. There I hope to find out about Lydia.

I board a truck full of people. We drive alongside twisted iron beams which once held the Central Station on Jerozolimska Street and turn left to Marszalkowska, the main street of Warsaw. In a daze, I look at the scenes unrolling before my eyes. Am I dreaming? Is this mass of rubble really Warsaw? I can barely recognize the places where I once knew every stone.

The driver turns onto Krolewska Street and drives along the serpentine street of Karowa, and descends toward the Vistula River. All the regular bridges have been destroyed. A narrow pontoon bridge is the only way across. We ease over it, and the truck stops on the right bank. After a few minutes, I am in front of the Search Committee office.

An old servant opens the door. "There is nobody in the office yet," he says. "They arrive at nine o'clock. You may sit down in the waiting room." I wait the longest hour of my life. A big clock ticks monotonously. I put my head in my hands and close my eyes, trying to get some rest after the sleepless night, but the tension prevents me from dozing off. I stand up and pace the room.

When the clerks arrive, the old man leads me to a room full of files. A young woman, her hair tied back neatly in a bun, sits at a desk. She seems so competent, so self-assured. This is the moment I have waited for. I write a description and personal data about Lydia on a slip of paper, and hand it to the woman without saying a word. She looks at me, nods curtly, and takes out a box of cards. I watch her fingers leafing through the cards. They blur before my eyes. I am sweating. My fists are clenched. She does not raise her eyes. Only the sound of shuffling cards interrupts the silence.

"No." That's all I hear. My head turns aside as if struck. I see darkness.

I walk the streets of Warsaw, not knowing where I am or where I am going. People bump into me and say, "Ah, this is another crazy one."

I hear myself speak: "Where is my wife? Where is my family? Where is little Misia, the beautiful, innocent child?"

I suffer more now than in the hell of the concentration camps. Then I could hope that the suffering would end and a new life would begin. Then I knew I would never see my family again, except, I hoped, my wife. Now I know I will be absolutely alone. No one will echo my words. No one will understand them. I will toss in bed through sleepless nights, and walk alone in the day, surrounded by cold, distant faces, blank and uncaring.

I find myself standing on the shore of the Vistula River, watching the broad river as it rolls by, its grey waves eternally breaking. "Tell me," I yell at the river, "what word of my parents did the wind bring to you while the ghetto was burning? What were the words and the prayers uttered by hundreds of thousands of innocent victims of this city?"

The river says nothing. The waves are silent.

I walk through the ruined city, from one heap of rubble to another. I stop at the once grand Marshal's Square. As a small child, I played here on the grounds of a big Russian church. Later the church was destroyed and the square rebuilt. On one side stood the monument to Prince Poniatowski, on the other, the Hotel Europejski, once the best hotel in Warsaw. The terrace of the hotel was the meeting place of Warsaw's elite — politicians, diplomats, financiers, and high-ranking officers. A table was reserved for "the colonels," the actual rulers of the country. In summer, I used to go to the little garden in the hotel courtyard. In winter, elegant couples danced at the "Ball of Fashion" in the grand hall. Now gloomy, dark holes gape back at me from places where doors and windows used to be.

I walk out from the hotel to another big square and stumble over a fallen street lamp. Passing a mountain of rubbish, I approach the ruins of the palace which once housed the Ministry of Foreign Affairs. I remember scenes that took place in front of that building: the visits of the British General Ironside, and the ministers of foreign affairs — Ciano of Italy, Ribbentrop of Germany, and Beck of Poland who would arrive in a long black car, sporting a top hat. On the third of September, 1939, I stood in a crowd in front of the British Embassy. The sun shone brightly on that Sunday. After two days of bombing, the German planes temporarily stopped flying over Warsaw. The news came that England and France had declared war. Frantic crowds chanted, "*Do Berlina! Do Berlina!* To Berlin! To Berlin!" The British Ambassador appeared on the balcony. "We will fight, arm in arm, until victory," he called out. Such boundless enthusiasm. All that was a long time ago.

Turning left, I pass by the burnt-down Kronenberg Palace and the Museum of Art. I enter the once fashionable Mazowiecka street. On my left are the ruins of the coffeehouse, Ziemianska, once a hot spot for gossip and witty conversations. A couple of tables on the mezzanine were always reserved for the poets — Tuwim, Slonimski, Lechon, Hemar — *habitués* of the place. Their songs, poems and satires captured the life of the city. I remember a cabaret actor who performed a number called "Little Mustache," mocking Hitler, who seemed just an overblown buffoon.

I pick my way through the rubble covering the streets. Small carts stand idly by, ready to remove the debris, but no one is working. I maneuver through piles of beams and rafters, over puddles of dirty water. A startled rat runs in front of me from under a beam. Behind a tangle of wires, I recognize the place where I used to play tennis with my friend, Ignas. Standing there, I see myself playing on a bright, sunny day before the war.

Oh, how full of energy I am. Ignas, tall and athletic, is a master at playing near the net. Aware of his tactics and his strong backhand, I do my best to force him away from the net. I lob with my forehand and chase him to the corners. Now I will finish him off, I think, as I suddenly change the rhythm of play and charge the net. But Ignas is faster. He returns my ball with his strong backhand. "Hell!" I can't reach it. Ignas wins. We both wipe the sweat from our faces, laughing.

Ignas was my best friend. I loved him like a brother. He impressed me with his intelligence and imagination, and I delighted in our conversations. How many nights we spent walking the streets of sleeping Warsaw, discussing everything from literature and art to sports, politics and women. Ignas would talk about his philosophy of life or describe his latest amorous conquests. Although he was not good-looking, he cut a very attractive figure. He dressed impeccably in English tweeds and exuded a rugged masculinity. Widely read, a dazzling conversationalist, and an endless source of gossip, he always spoke of subjects that interested his listener.

I was shy, especially with women, until I met Ignas. He coached me in the art of dressing well. Then he would present me to women as "the best-dressed man in Warsaw." His own successes with women always amazed me. Young or old, aloof or approachable, they all found him irresistible. He was married, but he had no qualms about his indiscretions. On Sundays, he would stroll with his pretty wife, Helka, along Warsaw's fashionable Mazowiecka Street. They were a striking couple — he, tall and elegant; Helka, petite and stylish.

How I dream of hearing his voice again, but I know I never will. Ignas was caught and taken to Pawiak Prison, where he was shot for insubordination. He had charmed his way out of many close scrapes, but not his final encounter with the Gestapo.

I leave Mazowiecka Street and approach Napoleon Square. On my left is the former Central Post Office, on my right the building of an insurance company, the only skyscraper in prewar Warsaw. Only its blackened walls remain. On the square, which once thronged with life, there is not one living soul. I pass the Philharmonic House. In an adjacent building, there was a lending library, and across the street, a vast and fascinating bookstore. As a boy, I used to stand in front of the window studying the titles on the books displayed, imagining the stories within.

I come to the place of the once fashionable night club, Adria. Pictures from the past flash before my eyes. Elegant men and women once graced this place. Did they realize then that they were dancing on a volcano? How many of them are still alive?

I turn to the main street, Marszalkowska. At the corner of Swietokrzyska Street is the place where I was born. There is no trace of the house, only high weeds and unkempt grass. I turn to Wielka Street and reach the apartment building where my family lived. I stand and stare at the ruins of our home. On the level of our third floor apartment, a few stray bricks held together by rods of iron are swinging in the wind. I recognize the outlines of the rooms, some tiles, the remains of a stove. I envision the placement of the furniture in the rooms as it stood six years ago. My memories are so intense that I nearly lose all sense of the present. It seems to me that here is the only place on earth where my soul can speak to my parents.

I am sixteen years old, hurrying home from school. For my birthday, my parents have bought me a bookcase filled with an illustrated ten-volume encyclopedia and books of the classic German writers. I am eager to feel the green covers of the books with their gold embossed titles, and then to read each one, starting with my beloved poet, Heinrich Heine.

In fifteen minutes I reach my home in the center of Warsaw. On the ground floor of the building is my parents' store, where they sell piece goods and silk flowers. My father imports the goods and my mother runs the store, assisted by my aunt and two salesgirls. I don't see my mother in the store, so I run up the stairs to the workshop, where she is showing one of the young women how to make a rose from red silk. She is a good teacher and makes sure her pupil understands each intricate step. With six people making flowers, the room is buzzing with activity. My mother notices me at the door and smiles.

The door of my father's office is ajar. He sits there with two friends in the small back room, discussing some philosophical problem. He is a handsome man with a sensitive, thoughtful face, and expressive eyes. He is always surrounded by intellectuals and admirers, and is much more interested in literature and the arts than in business, unlike my mother, who loves enterprise. On another day, I might slip in unobtrusively to listen to my father's conversation, but today I cannot wait to see my books.

I climb another flight of stairs to our apartment on the third floor. I run to the bedroom I share with my brother and grandmother. The new bookcase stands in a corner. I take out a book by Heine and turn to a favorite poem:

> Im wunderschönen Monat Mai,
> Als alle Knospen sprangen,
> Da ist in meinem Herzen
> Die Liebe aufgegangen.
>
> Im wunderschönen Monat Mai,
> Als alle Vögel sangen,
> Da hab'ich ihr gestanden
> Mein Sehnen und Verlangen.

> *In the wonderful month of May,*
> *When all buds were opening,*
> *In my heart then*
> *Love was born.*
>
> *In the wonderful month of May,*
> *When all the birds were singing,*
> *I confessed to her*
> *My yearning and my desire.*

At two o'clock, it is time for lunch, the main meal of the day. Lunch is served from eleven o'clock because there are so many mouths to feed in our household: my parents, my grandmother, my aunt, my brother, my twin sister, myself, a young governess, a cook, a maid, two salesgirls, and six women from the shop.

My brother, Maurice, who is three years older than I, and my twin sister, Edwarda, come home from school and join us at the table. My brother cracks some jokes and everybody laughs. He has a wonderful sense of humor and a great imagination, which he often uses for inventing pranks. One night, he tied a string to the leg of my grandmother's bed. My grandmother went through her elaborate ritual of getting undressed, peeling off her several blouses, one after another, until only one remained. Then, rubbing the front of her body, she climbed into bed. But the bed started to move! Maurice was pulling it with a string to the middle of the room. "Rascal, good for nothing," she scolded.

Another day, my brother convinced my sister and me to be his maid and valet. My job was to help him with his overcoat, and hers to open the door. He said he would pay us once a week. We worked for him a week and at the end we got nothing. We were angry, but not for long. We knew my brother had a heart of gold, and it was impossible to resist his charm.

As we eat, I hear my parents coming up the stairs. My father is arguing with my mother about the bookkeeping. "Cesia," he says — his nickname for Cecilia — "why can't you just write everything down when it happens? When you pay a bill, write it down. When there is a new order, simply make a notation in the proper place. It's so much more reliable."

"Max, I am busy during the day, so I write everything down in the evening. You know I have a good memory. Why do you get so upset?"

It is true that my mother has an amazing memory. She can repeat word for word a long conversation with anyone, but she cannot remember a name. "What is your name, sir?"

she would ask a customer in her charming way. "Goldberg," the man replies. "Well, Mister Slowik..." she continues immediately.

I don't like it when my parents argue, but they never stay angry for long. "Sometimes I get so angry at your father," my mother says to me, "but then I say to myself: 'Look at this man's face, honesty is written all over it. How can I not love such a man?'"

My mother's friendly face breaks into a smile. Her whole demeanor expresses warmth and inspires confidence. I admire my mother — her optimism, her charm, her energy and, above all, her special gift for understanding people. She can just look at someone with her sensitive grey eyes, and read their heart and mind.

I am just finished eating as my parents are sitting down. Without asking permission, I quietly try to escape back to my new books, but my mother motions me to sit down again and join the family conversation. Sulking, I sit, but refuse to take part. After all, this is my birthday. I should receive special treatment. When the ordeal is finally over, my mother takes my hands in hers and says, "Do not be so impatient with us, Henryk. Time goes by so quickly, and soon you will be a grown man. Perhaps you will study in Paris or live in some distant country. Then you will remember these times, my son, and you will ask: 'Mother, where are you?'"

Oh, yes, mother, where are you? Why am I left alone to grieve for you? Why didn't I die, too? The iron rods wave at me from the rubble, mocking my agony.

Everyone in my family is gone. They are all dead. There is not even a grave to hold their bones.

"Their grave is in my heart," I say aloud, "in my memory, in these very words."

Not far from where I stand is the apartment where Lydia lived with her parents. I walk slowly through the heaps of bricks, but cannot find the building in the rubble. Finally, a fragment of what was once a balcony helps me identify the place.

I will live with their memories and speak to their shadows. I will tell them, "My place is with you."

"No!" a voice inside me cries. "I do not believe that my wife is no longer alive. I will not believe it unless I have absolute proof of her death. It doesn't matter that I haven't found her yet. She may be sick somewhere. Only four months have passed since the end of the war."

But another voice whispers ominously, "Of every ten men in the concentration camps, only one survived; of ten women, only one. The chance of you both surviving is perhaps one in a hundred. Be realistic. Why should fate favor you?"

Estonia

FROM VAIVARA we are taken to Goldfields, another labor camp in eastern Estonia, some seventy miles west of Leningrad. In the small hours of the morning, we stand in five long rows as the Lagerführer *passes in front of us. I am behind Dworzecki and Rosenblatt, in front of Czertok. As the* Lagerführer *comes closer, I recognize him from Vaivara, where I worked as an attendant at a military gas station. He would stop for gasoline, each time repeating the same German pun, "If you don't do it well, you'll be hit on your ass, and only ashes will become of you." I would answer smartly, clicking my heels in the Prussian manner: "Jawohl, Herr Lagerführer. Now please sign this receipt for gasoline." He would call me impudent for asking him to sign a receipt, but I would insist that I had my orders and had to follow them.*

Now he is inspecting our rows. "I am going to appoint the Lagerältester, *foreman of the camp," he announces in German. He walks along slowly, and when he notices me, he stops. "You, come here," he says.*

I step forward and click my heels. Three thousand pairs of eyes are staring at me.

"Where do I know you from?"

"I am the gasoline attendant from Vaivara."

"Ach ja. *You are the impudent guy who always wanted receipts. I appoint you now the* Lagerältester."

Lagerältester? *My mind reels as I think of what this would mean: a full stomach, a separate room, exemption from heavy work, and virtually unlimited power over three thousand people, the power of an Oriental prince. How easy life could be!*

Then, I think of what my mother always told me. "Henryk, never strive for power over other men. It will twist you into something ugly."

"Ich bedaure, *I regret,* Herr Lagerführer, *I am not the right man."*

"Gut, abtreten. *All right, step back,"* he says, slightly piqued. *I return to my place, a nobody again.*

Later, I am surrounded by my friends.

"You did the right thing," says Dworzecki. "I am proud of you," adds Czertok.

I bask all day in the admiration of several of the pretty women of our camp: sweet Lotte, Gretl, and the glamorous Elizabeth of Prague.

In Estonia, Dworzecki, Rosenblatt, Czertok and I vow to live like brothers. Each one will bring whatever he can to our community of four, and we will share all acquisitions as common property. We vow to sustain and protect each other. We are unique in the jungle of camp life.

Rosenblatt, at 50, is the oldest in the group. Dworzecki, Czertok, and I are all thirty-five. Czertok, a teacher, and Dworzecki, a physician, are both from Vilno. In our partnership, Czertok performs the functions of cook and valet. He knows how to make excellent dishes, how to start a fire in the field, how to sew and mend, and has many other practical skills of everyday life. Dworzecki takes care of our health. Sometimes, when he is compensated by other inmates for medical ministrations, he proudly brings back an extra piece of bread or a few spoons of soup. "Esculapia," he calls it. I function as a so-called "organizer." I dart into a field on our way to work, pull up some carrots or beet roots, and quickly run back to line before the Estonian guards notice. Sometimes the guards shoot, but it doesn't discourage me since they are always slow. But, by far, our main provider is Rosenblatt. Because he can speak the language, he trades directly with the Estonians and brings back bread, meat, or fat.

Men and women live together in the camps in Estonia. The women usually manage better than the men. They know how to cook and sew, how to keep their bodies clean. Many of them manage to look attractive, while most of the men are neglectful. Sex does not have much place in the imagination of the camp inmates. Our bodies want only food, sleep, and freedom from lice.

When a dangerous epidemic of typhus broke out in Vaivara, I was isolated in a common room with other men and women, away from the rest of the camp. Some of the women were beautiful. We lived together, dressed and undressed in the same room, but our relationships were innocent. The idea of a sexual encounter simply never occurred to us.

What erotic life there is in Estonia is concentrated around the kitchen. The cook, who steals a good part of our rations, has his own harem of women. Anyushka, the Lagerführer's *lover, also works in the kitchen. She is a saucy young Jewish woman from Kovno. She wears glaring make-up and silk stockings, and often stands in front of the kitchen, her hand resting defiantly on her hip, showing off her well-fed body and jutting breasts. An impudent smile on her full lips seems to say: "Beggars, you can look at me, but you can't touch."*

Returning to camp after a day of heavy work, exhausted, aching with hunger, sometimes carrying a dying man, we inhale the intoxicating vapors wafting from the kettles of soup, and look at Anyushka. A few, stronger than the others, ravish her provocative body with their eyes. You bitch, you German's whore, others think, as Anyushka turns back to the kitchen, her round posterior undulating above her shapely legs.

Most of the camp dignitaries have lovers. They carry on their affairs amid the dismal scenery of the camps. When we go to sleep in the big common room, the Blockaelteste, *Hans, a former actor from Vienna, frequently roams the room, pinching and grabbing the backsides of the young boys. In their lust, those in power prostitute women and young boys for a piece of bread or a plate of soup.*

Twelve-year-old Berele has a beautiful voice and often performs his repertoire of songs for us in the big room on Sunday nights. The talented Berele is also a "Lustknabe," or lover-boy, of the camp commandant Hengst. But when Hengst is about to leave Estonia, he does not hesitate to send his beloved Berele, along with the boy's father, to death in a mass execution.

One evening, a hundred women arrive at the gate of the camp. With their shaven heads, they look like ghosts. Only a fortnight before, they were in their homes in Hungary. The deportations started all over the country suddenly and unexpectedly. Thousands of Hungarian Jews were evacuated, mostly to Auschwitz, where they were greeted by the chimneys of the crematoria spitting out billows of dark smoke. Some groups, like these women, were lucky. They were separated from the majority who remained in Auschwitz and sent to remote places.

After a few days, the Hungarian women are integrated into the routine of camp life. I become friendly with two sisters from Kolozsvar. They are eighteen years old, tall, pretty, and well-mannered. They look so alike that I often cannot distinguish one from the other. "I am Alice," one will say. "I am Klara," says the other. Sometimes they fool me. "I am Klara," Alice will say. After a few minutes, they reveal the truth with gales of laughter.

Alice and Klara are the grandnieces of the famous American film magnate, Adolph Zukor. "Do you know who he is?" they ask.

"Oh, yes," I reply. "I saw his name many times on the screen, 'Paramount Pictures, Adolph Zukor and Jesse Lasky present....' Your granduncle's millions can't help you now. He should have brought you to the United States before the war."

Alice looks forlorn, so I try to change her mood. "But let's forget where we are for the moment. Please, sing a czardas *for me."*

I listen, entranced, as they sing. There is so much life in their voices. For a while, we are all transported to a puszta *where the Hungarian peasants dance, and we forget our miserable circumstances.*

"Aren't all the peasant dances really Gypsy music?" I ask.

"No, they are mostly Hungarian, Romanian and Russian tunes that the Gypsies hear in the villages," Alice explains. "They learn them even without the written notes because they have music in their blood." Alice speaks animatedly. Her excitement brings roses to her cheeks.

"And is it true that the song, 'Szomoru Vasarnap, Gloomy Sunday,' was banned in Budapest? I read once that

after listening to the plaintive tones and lyrics, many lovers committed suicide."

"Yes, it's true," says Klara. "At least those were the newspaper accounts in those days." Klara begins singing the song in Hungarian, while Alice translates the lyrics for me:

> *On that gloomy Sunday I waited for you.*
> *Long into the night did I wait.*
> *And when the stars and the moon*
> *Began fading in the sky,*
> *I sighed: "All in vain."*
> *Sobs choked my throat*
> *And at dawn life seemed*
> *Aimless and without meaning.*

"Strange," I wonder aloud. "It seems such a romantic luxury to kill oneself because of an unrequited love affair. Can you imagine committing suicide, Klara?"

"Certainly not now. No one thinks of suicide in this camp, despite the terrible conditions. Before, we would never have believed that we would still want to live in such circumstances. Yet, we want to survive."

"That's true," I agree. "I know of only three cases of suicide in the camps. Before the war, you could often read about people committing suicide. Yet, even those who considered themselves poor then were immensely rich compared to us. For us, a slice of bread is the greatest of luxuries. All around us, there are children who have lost their parents, parents who have lost their children, husbands and wives who have lost their spouses, and they all still want to live. Why is the instinct to live so powerful?"

Alice sighs. "Please, Henryk, let us drop this dismal subject. We sang for you. Do the same for us."

"All right." *I remember a song which I heard once at the* Folies Bergères *in Paris. A man wearing a grey top hat and carrying a cane under his arm sang it to the Dolly sisters who looked exactly alike, and wore the same scanty wraps.* "Here it is:"

>Elles ont les mêmes nez,
>les mêmes yeux étonnés,
>La même bouche et les deux oreilles pareilles.
>Oh, quelle merveille!
>
>Un soir, lorsqu'il faisait noir,
>dans le corridor,
>j'en ai pris une et je l'ai embrassée bien fort.
>Elle m'a rendu mon baiser,
>seulement dans l'obscurité,
>je me demandais tout anxieux:
>"Laquelle est-ce des deux?"
>
>*They have the same nose,*
>*the same surprised eyes*
>*the same mouth, and ears alike.*
>*It's a miracle!*
>
>*One dark night,*
>*in the corridor,*
>*I met one of them and kissed her passionately.*
>*She kissed me, too.*
>*But in the darkness,*
>*I asked myself anxiously:*
>*"Which of the two is she?"*

Klara laughs. "But such a romance could not happen between you and us."

The Aftermath

"Why?" I ask facetiously. "Who knows how many days we will live? Why not take from life what still can be taken? Klara? Alice?"

"I am sure," says Klara, "that more important things are on your mind."

Klara takes her mess kit and produces a piece of bread. "Take it, Henryk."

"Oh, no, Klara. I would be a scoundrel to accept a part of your ration. I brought you soup yesterday because I happened to get two portions. The cook made a mistake."

"Liar. The cook never makes mistakes. Take the bread or you'll offend us."

"Hello, hello. What are you arguing about?" Rosenblatt bustles up, full of cheer. "Look what I have!" He opens his bag and takes out a whole loaf of bread and a large piece of lard.

"Don't quarrel over trifles. I have bartered my gold ring with an Estonian guard and this is what I got. I invite you for supper, all of you."

"Leiba, leiba!" the twins scream. "Leiba" is the most important word in the camp. It means "bread" in Estonian.

We fill our stomachs. Heaven!

"Thank you, thank you." The twins kiss Rosenblatt on both cheeks.

The brothers Di Ponte, two coachmen from Vilno, are kings of the camp. Before the war they took pleasure in stealing. They are both very strong. On the first day of our arrival at Vaivara, they offered their services to the SS, who need such men to maintain discipline through terror.

One of their duties is to carry out camp punishments, which include twenty-five paddles for minor offenses. Frenzl, the younger brother, holds the delinquent by twisting his

~ 86 ~

hands behind his back and trapping the head between his knees. Sholemke, the nastier of the two, beats the offender with a big stick. The Lagerführer *stands a few paces away, a cigarette in the corner of his mouth, tapping lightly at the tips of his highly polished black shoes with his riding crop. These displays take place during roll-call and leave us feeling helpless and disgusted. It never occurs to us to resist the Di Pontes, which would only result in more painful blows and additional punishment by the* Lagerführer.

One day my spirits are lifted by the news that the Allies have taken Rome. Sholemke Di Ponte is working his stick even harder than usual this day and, as people return from work, he orders them to carry heavy bags of potatoes. A burning hatred seethes within me, and when Sholemke approaches me with his order, I refuse. He grabs the flaps of my coat with one hand and brandishes his stick with the other.

I feel an intense desire to bite Sholemke's throat. Without thinking, I strike. My left fist hits Sholemke's broad jaw, followed by a right to his stomach. Both blows are so unexpected and sudden that he does not understand what has happened. He loses his balance, and seizes his belly with both hands. I give vent to my pent-up anger and hatred, and before Sholemke can straighten up, I batter him with blows. "Take that, you scoundrel, you son of a whore, you dog's shit," I scream. We are surrounded by a large circle of inmates, gathered to see David take on Goliath. Blood runs into Sholemke's eyes and blinds him. I punch him again in the face.

Suddenly I feel a terrible blow on my back. Frenzl has hit me with a shovel as hard as he could. The excited crowd separates us.

For weeks after this event, Dworzecki regularly puts his ear to my back to listen for a hum in my lungs. In spite of the pain, which lasts many weeks, I always think of this event with delight. The Di Ponte brothers do not report the incident to the Lagerführer. *They probably do not want him to know that their prestige has been challenged. And they never bother me again. But I soon realize how lucky I was. I become too weak to fight like that again, and must restrain my Polish vanity and pride. Survival takes strength, I learn, but it also takes cunning, timing, and luck.*

From the time I learned that Lydia is alive in Riga, I have been trying to send word to her. Finally, I get the chance to send a letter with a Dutch laborer who is being sent back to Holland by way of Riga. Soon after, the Red Army breaks the German flanks between Leningrad and Narva, and the Germans begin evacuating the camps of Eastern Estonia.

Only Two Remain

OUR TRAIN HAS BEEN STANDING *for hours at the railroad station. For two days we've been travelling around, and the Germans still don't know what to do with us. They have already taken us by train to the port of Tallinn, but there were no ships to transport us to Germany. Our train returned inland to a station in the vicinity of the Kloga camp.*

Dworzecki knows that his wife and sister are in that camp. I ask my friend if he looks forward to being reunited with them. At first, he does not reply. Finally he says, "My greatest desire is to be with my wife and sister. But not now, not under these circumstances. It may be better for us to be reunited when we are free, if we survive."

The train moves at last. We do not get off in Kloga. We hear that there is not room enough in the crowded camp for new prisoners. We move on.

We pass through Tallinn again, and about twenty kilometers further, stop in a field. We get off the train surrounded by SS men and Estonian soldiers, and are ordered to lie on the ground. We spend the night under the open sky, lying on blankets. Stars twinkle and the moon casts its shimmering light as it gazes down on the demented dwellers of the planet Earth.

Finally, we are taken on the ship Stadt Stettin from Tallinn to Gdansk, and from there to the concentration camp, Stutthof.

Stutthof is a large camp with about 60,000 prisoners. Men's and women's barracks are separated by a double row of barbed wire. It is strictly forbidden to approach the wires. The only place where it is possible to exchange a few words with a woman, if she happens to be on the other side at the same time, is behind the kitchen. To get there, it is necessary to have a job in the kitchen. I manage to get such a job removing garbage. This gives me the opportunity to get close to the wires. Then, whenever I see a woman behind the wire, I ask if she knows my wife.

After many attempts, I speak to a woman who has come from the Kaiserwald camp near Riga, and who knew Lydia there. She tells me that Lydia received my letter, and that she tried to escape, but was caught after several days. She says Lydia will probably be coming to Stutthof soon, because all the inmates in Kaiserwald are being evacuated. From that day on, I wait anxiously for my wife's arrival, imagining the day I will give her the gift I have hidden in the heel of my shoe.

I remember the rainy day in Vaivara camp in Estonia when I bartered for the necklace with a Jewish astronomer from Vilno.

"How much?" I asked.

"Five rations of bread and ten cigarettes."

"What? You must be crazy!"

"Look, these are real pearls from Bahrain on the Persian Gulf. I paid a fortune for this necklace in Paris."

"This is not Paris. This is Estonia. If I give you five rations, I'll starve to death. You don't want me to die, do you?"

"Don't be silly. You have friends — Czertok, Doctor Dworzecki, Doctor Rosenblatt. Each of them will help you a little."

"Stop kidding. Who would give away his bread? You are an astronomer, so you ask an astronomical price."

"Look, I'll be frank with you. I have no use for these pearls. My wife is dead. But this is my last offer: three rations of bread and five cigarettes. Take it or leave it."

I looked at the necklace. The pearls were small and white, without a blemish, and perfectly matched in size. They reflected the light of the sun in little rainbows. They were amazingly iridescent. I imagined them gleaming around Lydia's lovely neck as we danced.

"All right, I'll take them. I'll pay you in installments over four weeks."

The pearls enchanted me. What a wonder, I thought, that an oyster irritated by a particle of sand can produce a thing of such beauty. Some day, if I survive, I will give these pearls to Lydia.

That evening, after working in the fields, I went to see Mendel, the shoemaker. "Mendel, you are my friend. Please help me. I will give you a ration of bread. You see these pearls? I want you to hide them in my shoe with a small photograph."

Mendel nodded. He looked at the pearls and the shoe, then took his treasured tools from a bag and set to work. He carved a hole in the heel of the shoe. He wrapped the precious pearls together with a small picture I had managed to save of my parents, and put them in the hole. He then covered the hole with leather and rubber.

From that time, the shoes and I have become inseparable. They are on my feet all day and next to my head at night. I have rescued them in countless situations, but the most dangerous one happens in Stutthof.

We are ordered to enter the showers, mouths open, while the guards check whether we are hiding anything. One guard puts his fingers in our mouths, and another guard probes deep up our rectums. While we are waiting for our turn, Rosenblatt swallows three diamonds he has managed to save, planning to retrieve them later in his excrement. He does not know then that everyone would have to relieve themselves under the watchful eye of a Kapo.

My trouble begins at the shower. We are ordered to leave our clothes and shoes in heaps, then to pick others at random afterwards. Although I remember exactly what my shoes look like, I cannot find them in the enormous piles. I have to take some other shoes.

Over the next few days, I carefully examine everyone's footwear. Finally I notice my shoes on a young man's feet. That night, he is so light-minded as to leave the shoes under his bed. Waiting until it is relatively quiet, I sneak over in the darkness and grab them, leaving my new ones in their place. I return to my bunk and place the shoes beside the rag on which I lay my head. Luck is with me, and the pearls and I are reunited.

Rosenblatt's luck takes a turn for the worse in Stutthof. He is beaten badly, and his wounds become infected. A few pills of prontosil could save him, but there is no way to get even one. Since anyone suspected of a serious illness is a doomed man, we keep Rosenblatt's condition secret.

In September of '44, two days before Lydia's transport is supposed to arrive, Dworzecki, Rosenblatt and I are sent to the Dautmergen concentration camp, near the Swiss border. Czertok remains behind.

Rosenblatt's condition deteriorates, and he is covered with pus. The odor is unbearable. After a journey of four days in a cattle train, we arrive at a little station in Germany close to the French and Swiss borders. Dworzecki and I each take Rosenblatt by the arm and, covering our nose with our other hand, drag him from the station to Dautmergen. It is September, and the fruit trees along the road are heavy with apples and pears. Piles of fruit lie on the ground under the trees. We have had nothing to eat or drink during the journey, and feast our greedy eyes on the fruit. One man cannot resist and runs to pick some apples. A shot. The man falls.

As we continue to drag Rosenblatt along, I think of his many talents. He was an erudite professor of physics with an amazing breadth of knowledge. He would often recite poems for us. He would identify the stars in the sky. Through several camps he boosted our spirits, and was the best provider of our group.

I remember the evening he recited a poem by the Hebrew poet, Chaim Bialik, written after a pogrom in Kiev:

> The revenge for the blood
> Of even one small child,
> The devil himself has not invented yet.
> Let the spilled blood sink
> Into the depth of the earth
> And penetrate its darkness.
> Let it undermine the foundation of the land.

The pus never stops oozing from Rosenblatt's poor, sick body and, after another two weeks, he dies.

Now, of the four friends, only Dworzecki and I remain.

Writings

MY STAY IN WARSAW is exhausting. Every step brings such painful memories that I can no longer bring myself to look at the shattered remnants of my youth. How can I remain here among these ruins? To go on living, I have to leave this graveyard of the past.

I take a train to Berlin. There I trudge from office to office looking for information, but find no trace of Lydia. After a few days, I go to Magdeburg.

The camp near the Polta factory is like most other camps I have seen — barracks, barbed wire, and a large square in the center where I imagine Lydia standing for the interminable roll calls. The factory is deserted now. I find several survivors living in Magdeburg who knew Lydia in the camps. One suggests that if Lydia survived, she might have gone to France with one of the French women in the camp who was her friend.

As I walk the streets of Magdeburg, the same persistent question keeps churning in my mind: Did Lydia escape on this very street, or did a bullet end her last attempt for freedom, one day before liberation?

After a long, tiresome journey by freight train and on foot, I arrive back in Munich on a grey morning. Another month passes. By now I am fully recovered physically, but my will is as shattered as the rubble of Warsaw.

One of my American friends suggests, "Why don't you write? You should describe your experiences."

I do not like the idea. Why should I ruminate even more about the past? I will never stop thinking about what happened, but writing about it means analyzing each detail, asking questions to which there are no replies.

"Why should I?" I ask.

"Because you are a victim and witness to this great tragedy. The memoirs of survivors are crucial historical testimonies."

I consider his words and come to believe that he is right. As difficult as it may be, it is my obligation to write about what happened — my duty to the memory of those who died, and to future generations. I contemplate the magnitude of the task. How can words describe what I have experienced?

Later that night, I sit down and write:

> Millions and millions of stars and planets, guided by an invisible hand, rotate in the infinity. Space and motion move the eternal pendulum of time.
>
> One of the planets, Earth, revolves around the sun. The continuous revolution causes lightness and darkness, heat and cold, seasons and years — millions of years.
>
> An invisible hand creates life: first microbes, then animals. One of the animals, man, looks up at the stars. "I do not understand," he thinks. "I want to understand."

The Aftermath

Man's mind changes the surface of the earth. He asks again: "What is the purpose of life, what is the aim of everything around me?"
"Happiness," replies the soul.

"Happiness? Ah, yes, my happiness," says the man, killing a fellow man and enslaving another.

"I know the truth," says the first noble man. "Do not do unto your neighbor what you would not have him do unto you."

On this planet there is a bit of land called Europe, surrounded on three sides by water. It has a mild climate, rich soil, and a coastline that favors navigation.

In the middle of Europe, Germany. Where there once stood dense forests inhabited by bears and wolves, there are now towns and idyllic little villages.

Near the towns and villages are wires — barbed wires, electrified wires. Behind the wires are live skeletons with emaciated faces and burning eyes. Hunger wrenches their bellies. Lice cover their skin.

Death is everywhere around them. Not death, the redeemer, who gently closes eyelids with his velvety fingers, then guides one to the great mystery beyond. But death who jabs with sharp, claw-like fingers while it laughs its hideous laugh.

People are dying. Nooses tighten around their necks, shots rip through their brains, gas macerates their lungs.

What are the last thoughts of the dying? What are their last words?

They say: "Do not forget!"

I read what I have written and realize it is too abstract. Perhaps I am still too close to the horror I have lived through. But where will I ever find the words that could describe this tragedy?

I think of my father and how he would write and rewrite, struggling to express what he wanted to say. I decide I will have to try again. But not now.

I try to convince myself that Lydia is alive with her girlfriend somewhere in France, and I make arrangements to continue my search. Major Ordway helps me in every way he can. He introduces me to a French liaison officer who provides me with a document that will allow me to travel to France in a few weeks.

In the lonely days I spend in my room, I often think of my friend Marek Dworzecki. I wonder what happened to him and whether he is still alive. We owe our lives to each other. If not for our friendship, neither of us would have survived the camps. We were separated only one month before the end of the war, when I was sent to Dachau and he remained in Dautmergen. Before I was sent away, I asked another inmate to let him know that if I survived I would try to find him in Paris.

One evening I am reading *Our Word,* a Jewish newspaper published in Paris, and an article catches my eye. "How I Remained Alive." It is by Dr. Marek Dworzecki. I can hardly believe my eyes. He is alive! Thank you, oh God, thank you. I cannot contain my joy. It seems to me that I can hear my friend's voice as I read his words:

> Night. Jumbled thoughts allow me no peace. Memories will not leave me alone. I rise for a confession at midnight, like Jeremiah journeying in the night to the graves

of our fathers. I want to confess, to tell everything, but there is no one left to hear the prayer, "Take me under Thy wing, and be for me a mother and a sister." For my mother and sister, my friends and brothers, all sleep on the slopes of Ponary, the execution site in Vilno, in the mass graves of Estonia, in the German extermination camps.

I want to do penance, for the sin of having remained alive. I hear voices from beyond: "We did not survive, and you, you are still alive. How did you remain alive while we millions perished?" All their eyes are burning with the question.

I do not know, oh my conscience. I go crazy when I think about it. It was an inexplicable series of accidents, accident after accident. I always believed that I would live, that I would resist and survive. But those who were led to their execution also did not believe in their hearts' core that they were going on their last journey.

I saw death so many times in the ghetto and in the camps. I saw death eye to eye, face to face. Each time, salvation came, suddenly, as if by miracle. Each time a friend, a fellow in misery and suffering, supported me, offering an out-stretched hand, a good word, a few potatoes or a spoonful of soup during the endless days of hunger, a piece of glass to cool my head. And once, I shall never forget, when I was dying of a blood infection, my brother in the camps brought me life-saving medicine at the risk of his own life.

Dworzecki's article affects me profoundly. He and I were brothers in the camps. I prepare for my trip to France as in a dream, knowing that I will soon see him again. I fall asleep, my mind overwhelmed with memories.

One Morning

A SHRILL SOUND pierces my ears, interrupting the night's silence and awaking me from a stupor. Where am I? Who am I? Oh, yes, I am an inmate in the concentration camp, Dautmergen. It is the winter of '44. The bell is ordering us to get ready for a new day. A new day of fighting. Will I endure? Will I be able to survive all the dangers that lie in wait over the next seventeen hours until I can lie down again on this bed of boards? I rub my eyes and yawn. I see Dworzecki lying at my left. My body aches. A panicky thought flashes through my mind. The shoes! In one quick move, I reach under the mattress of wooden shavings. They are still there! Thank God! Every night a few pairs are stolen and anyone who can't find his in the morning has to go to work barefoot. We are ordered to leave our shoes under the beds at night, but no one follows this rule. We all sleep with our muddy shoes beside our head in order to protect them.

The menacing bell rings again, and the four hundred men in the hall begin to rise. "Aufstehen! Aufstehen! Get up!" scream the Blockschreiber *and his assistants. It is four in the morning.*

"Marek, get up," I say. I lift my head a little and hit the ceiling. It is very difficult to get dressed in this position, even with so little to put on. I sleep in my shirt and drawers. Over my drawers I slip on my blue and white striped pajama-like trousers. I wrap my feet in some rags and try to pull my shoes over them. I barely succeed because my feet are swollen and the pulling hurts. I curse and, with two ruthless tugs, get my feet into the shoes. From under the mattress I take two thick paper bags used for packing cement. I put one bag on my chest and one on my back, and tie them with small strings. I have a belt, thank heaven, which I bought from another inmate last week for a ration of bread. I put on my striped shirt. On the right side, there is a little red triangle and white stripe with a number so dirty it is illegible. On the trousers, above the right knee, the same illegible number is sewn.

"Steht auf, ihr Halunken! *Stand up, you sons of bitches!*" shout the assistants of the Blockaelteste. *I seize my little bag. All my treasures are in it. I tie my canteen to my belt, look at it and feel happy. Not everyone has a canteen like mine. It is made of aluminum, and has a cover, a genuine canteen of the* Wehrmacht. *I put on my cap and jump down from the third tier of beds. The hall is noisy with four hundred voices calling, cursing and moaning. The* Schreiber *runs around with a stick. He may suddenly emerge anywhere, and one must be careful to avoid being hit. In this respect Dworzecki and I have different philosophies. He thinks that when you see a stick you should run away as quickly as possible.*

"*I have told you a thousand times,*" he says, "*don't be too clever and don't wait until you are hit.*"

"*This is the psychology of a slave,*" I reply. "*When you see a stick, stand where you are and, instead of running, look carefully where the stick is moving. Then you'll be able to dodge away.*"

As I speak, I get hit across the chest with the stick, while Dworzecki escapes. He can see that the blow was not too hard and he laughs.

On the second tier of beds, the Stubenaelteste *distributes bread. The hall is divided into thirteen* Stuben *with an average of some thirty inmates each. The* Stubenaelteste *is a prisoner like all of us. His function is to distribute the rations in the morning and the evening and to see to the general order of his* Stube. *The* Stube *is a rather theoretical concept in our hall because there are no partitions between the* Stuben.

The distribution of the rations takes place in a dense crowd. Some jam and a loaf of bread are distributed to each group of five. This is the most important moment of the day. One of the five men cuts the bread for his group. He is someone who has a knife, and whom the others trust to divide the bread equally. Such knives are rare, and trustworthy people even more so. When the bread is cut into five parts, one of the five men turns his back, and another man points at a piece. "For whom?" he asks. "For the fourth man," is the random reply, and the fourth man gets that piece of bread. The finger points again, until all the lots are drawn. The difference between the slices may be only a few grams, but even these few grams are important. The system of drawing lots has been invented by the inmates so that only chance decides who gets a larger piece. The most desirable pieces are the heels of the bread, which always seem to be larger, although this might be an illusion. Everyone awaits the drawing of lots with excitement and anxiety, and the result can put one in a good or bad mood for hours. During the excitement of the draw, some stealing takes place and most of the inmates' treasures — little bags, canteens, cups, a potato — are lost at this time.

My ration of bread is not bad today. This puts me in a good mood. I have an understanding with Dworzecki. Each of us cuts his ration of bread into halves, keeping one for himself and giving one to the other. In this way we insure ourselves against the risk of either of us getting a smaller ration of bread on that day.

Now we have to move quickly. The chance to get the warm water called coffee is not at all certain. Blockaelteste Jurek expects the coffee to be distributed within ten minutes. After that everybody must leave the block immediately. Those who do not manage to get any coffee have to wait until the evening for something hot. We push, reach forward with our canteens and receive half a liter of liquid. We have to hurry out of the barracks because the Schreiber *is running amok with his stick.*

Outside, it is cool, dark and drizzling. The air is humid. An electric bulb in front of the barracks throws a pale, sickly yellowish light in which I can see the drops of rain. Bad. My good spirits vanish, despite my larger than usual portion of bread. I feel very unhappy. Where to go? Where to save myself from this rain, this insidious damp cold worse than frost? I have been on my feet for only half an hour and ahead of me is a long day. Our life is a fight, a constant struggle for survival. It is not a heroic fight, like that of an armed soldier, but the fight of victims whose only weapons are stubborn endurance and the will to survive. One has to be alert every moment in this fight to avoid each peril and exploit every opportunity for getting food.

I hold the canteen of warm coffee in one hand and the two halves of bread in the other. Now comes the blessed moment. I take a gulp of coffee. The warmth penetrates my stomach and spreads through my body. I put the bread to my mouth and take a bite. Oh, happiness! I can feel every gram giving me new life. This bread sustains my existence;

it gives me the strength with which to perform a thousand tasks today. Thanks to this bread I can stand on my feet and am able to think. I am happy as I eat, and yet, with every bite, I realize that my piece of bread is becoming smaller. I become uneasy. I know that I should save some bread for later or I will suffer through long hours of hunger. But I cannot resist. I eat and eat. One more bite, and then another. I do not want to think about what will be later.

"Did you eat all your bread?" I hear Dworzecki's voice.

"Go to hell," I reply, irritated.

I am angry now, deprived of the hope of eating another piece of bread later in the day. I will not have the joy of having a piece of happiness in my pocket during the long hours to come. Perhaps it is for the better, I try to console myself. What is in my stomach is mine and nobody can take it away. It would be worse if someone stole my bread. And I still have some potato peels. If we are lucky, we will have the chance to cook them in the field. My good spirits return.

Dworzecki is a man of strong will when it comes to eating. He can control himself much better than I. He was one of the few inmates in Stutthof who fasted on Yom Kippur, the Day of Atonement. *He gave me his plate of soup on that day. We were about to be evacuated to Germany, and the soup was exceptionally good. Months later, I still remember that soup. Dworzecki always cuts his ration of bread into small pieces. He eats one piece in the morning, and the others throughout the day. This system has the advantage of giving him moral support during the long hours of work, but the danger is that one of his pieces may be stolen or lost.*

The rain is pouring now and soaks us as we stand in the darkness in the big square. Almost every European nation is represented among us in the camp. The largest group are Poles, then Jews from Poland, Lithuania, Germany, and

France; then Russians, Ukrainians, Hungarians, Yugoslavs, Dutch, Belgians, Norwegians, French, Italians, Gypsies, and Germans. Common misery makes us equal. The conditions bring out national traits not evident before, particularly the trait of endurance. The Russians are the most resilient and able to adapt to the worst conditions. If they cannot walk, they crouch or crawl. The Jews come next, and then the Poles. The others are far behind. Frenchmen show little resilience, and the Gypsies are the most vulnerable of all.

It is five o'clock, the time when bartering and trading begin in a dozen languages.

"Who wants tobacco?"

"Who wants a knife?"

"Who wants a beetroot?"

A ration of bread — one fifth of a loaf on a good day, one seventh of a loaf or even less on a bad day — is the measure of all values.

"You," somebody says to me, "sell me your canteen. I'll give you a ration and a half."

I have no intention of selling my canteen, but I look at the bread and see that I am being offered a small piece. "Such a ration?" I say. "Find another fool."

"I'll also give you a beetroot."

"Go to hell."

A lot of turnips are sold. They are big and fill the stomach for an hour or two, dulling the ache of hunger. No one seems to consider the trouble involved in digesting them. Weak stomachs cannot tolerate raw cellulose, a cause of dysentery. Even more dangerous are the so-called "epelech." These are scraps and rinds left from apples that are crushed in a factory for juice. A group of inmates who work there sometimes bring the hard-to-digest scraps back to the camp and sell them at a low price. Dysentery in the camp is caused mainly by such efforts to appease our hunger.

The bell sounds again. Roll call. The Blockaelteste *and* Schreiber *of all the blocks come to the big square. The inmates fall into long rows, one row behind another. The ground on which we stand is wet and in some places the mud is ankle deep. Each step is an exertion because our boots stick in the mud. Often someone's boot gets so stuck that he has to pull his foot out of the boot, pull the boot out of the mud and put it back on his foot. Boots are our most precious treasure. Some of us wear wooden, rag-filled clogs. They are heavy and disintegrate after a short time. Most of us have swollen feet covered with sores. We stand on our feet seventeen hours a day, and march on long treks, so our sores never heal. With anemia, the sores get worse and produce pus.*

Not only my feet, but my whole body is covered with sores. There is no hope that they will heal, or even that the pus will stop oozing. I scratch my body with dirty hands, and the scabs tear off. Then I hold my bread in my pus-covered hands. I have not washed myself for six weeks. There is not enough water for drinking, let alone for washing. I try to wash myself in muddy puddles during work, but this always involves the risk of being noticed and beaten by a foreman, and getting even dirtier with the mud. When the snow comes, I can keep myself cleaner. I am continuously irritated by scores of lice that cover my body. There is no way of getting rid of them. Picking them off is simply an act of hopeless revenge. The optimists sometimes try to get rid of them by putting their lice-covered shirts on the hot stove pipes at night.

Dworzecki and I once tried to calculate how much blood the lice suck from each of us, and how much energy we lose by constantly scratching. It is difficult to decide which is more desirable — to be free of hunger or to be free of the irritation caused by these blood-sucking tiny monsters.

Two thousand people are scratching themselves, making contortions which under other conditions would seem comical. There is an odor of sweat, dirt, and pus. We are inured to the odor and pay attention only when the pus literally streams from the body, as it did with Rosenblatt.

The German command approaches. Young Kurt, "The Hare," and two other SS men are at the head. The voice of the Blockaelteste Jurek orders, "Augen... RECHTS! *Eyes to the right!* Augen gerade... AUS! *Eyes straight!* Muetzeeeee... en AUF! *Put on your caps!* Rührt euch! *At ease!* Vordermann und Seitenrichtung! *Look at the man in front of you; look at the man at your side!"*

We have been standing at the roll call for an hour and a half already. On my left is Schilperoordt, a Dutchman. I listen as he chants softly: "Hoe lang zal het nog duren, hoe lang zal het nog zijn, dat wij moeten arbeiden voor het zwijn van Berlijn! *How long will it last, how long will it be, that we will slave for the swine from Berlin?"*

"You're in good spirits," I say to him. "You probably ate well."

Schilperoordt laughs. "I used to eat well before the war," he says. "I was a butcher in Den Haag."

In the row in front of me, three Frenchmen stand arm-in-arm and sing softly: "Quand les oiseaux s'envolent.... *When the birds fly away...."* I like the lyric and the tune.

The roll call continues as the dawn breaks. Fragments of the overcast sky clear to reveal the first white rays of sun. Tired, I close my eyes. For the thousandth time, I consider the same questions. How many days have I been in the camps already? How many days if the war ends in, say, three months? Will it end by then? Will it ever end?

My thoughts jump to another subject, a scene from the past. I try not to think about it but I cannot stop myself. Lydia and I are in Vilno, a few months after our marriage and escape. We are having a slight disagreement. I want to hurt her, and refuse to eat the breakfast she has prepared. She puts rolls and butter, cheese, and wurst on the table. She pours the cocoa. The hot steam rises from the creamy, rich liquid in the cups.

"Henyu, drink the cocoa," she says. "Don't be silly."

But I maintain an offended air and pretend to read the newspaper. From the side of the paper, I watch what Lydia is doing. She cuts the rolls, spreads butter on the halves, and put slices of Swiss cheese between them. Then she goes to the kitchen and returns with a hot pan of scrambled eggs.

"I must stop thinking of this nonsense," I say to myself. I feel very bad. I swallow saliva and hear my empty stomach rumble. I open my eyes and try not to think of food anymore, but the temptation is too strong and the thoughts creep back again. I think of a variety of dishes. I count thirty kinds of pastry and twenty kinds of hors d'oeuvres. Potatoes can be cooked in twelve different ways. Let's be systematic: boiled potatoes, fried potatoes, mashed potatoes, potatoes with meat as in goulash, potatoes with beans and barley as in Jewish "choolent," potato knedels....

Oh, how bad! My stomach jumps to my throat. To eat! To eat! I want to eat!

Quiet! I will not surrender! I will stop dreaming about food.

*"*Arbeitskommandos formieren. *Align in groups to march to work," comes the command. The roll call is finally over.*

*We form groups, each to a different workplace. The groups stand at attention. "*Im Gleichschritt... marrrrrrsch.

March in equal step." We take each other's arm and, in ranks of five, pass through the camp gate.

"Eins, zwei, drei, vier. Eins, zwei, drei, vier. Links. *Left.* Links und links. Links. Links. Links und links."

We march on a highway. We turn to the left and pass what we call the Valley of Death where the corpses of the inmates are thrown into ditches. We march down a hill. The Kapo *and a few foremen are at the head of our group. SS guards are on each side. Somebody falls and stands up again, quickly. Faster! Quicker! My heart is beating hard. My lungs are straining. We climb a mountain. Faster! Faster!* "Wirst du laufen, du blöder Hund! *Will you run, you stupid dog!" One hour of marching is over. We arrive at the workplace.*

Dworzecki takes a shovel and I take a mattock. We are lucky today. We will not have to carry heavy rails, like yesterday, or push lorries loaded with stones. We will dig soft ground. Dworzecki and I position ourselves with a hill behind us. This way we can hardly be seen from afar, and we can spot anyone who is approaching. It is important to keep this strategic position for the whole day.

Our daily enemies — hunger, cold, lice and fatigue — are joined by one more: monotony. It is eight o'clock. We will remain here until five. Throughout the day we will count how many hours have passed already, and how many are still ahead. From time to time, someone will ask a foreman of the "Organization Todt" *what time it is, and his reply will be transmitted from man to man.*

When the work is not heavy, the inmates talk. The main topic is almost always food. We remember good times or discuss current issues of food: "How was yesterday's soup? How large was today's piece of bread? We also talk about our camp experiences, scenes of cruelty we have witnessed, and politics. We know what is happening in the world. A few inmates are "Kalefaktoren," servants in the rooms of SS, where they have the opportunity to read and, sometimes, even bring German newspapers into the camp. Political news spreads rapidly through the camp. Details of the current situation are analyzed and discussed. The progress of the Allied Armies is our hope and consolation. But we are troubled by the thought that even if some of us survive Germany's collapse, most will be killed at the last moment. In victory or defeat, we are doomed.

"Bewegung! Bewegung!" We hear the voice of a German guard. I start digging with much energy. The guard's presence forces us to do intensive work as long as he is around.

"You better work harder, you scoundrels, or you'll be taught a lesson, damn you," the guard growls.

As soon as he goes away, we relax.

I take off my shoe and check the heel carefully. "The pearls are still there," I say to myself. "Everything is in order." The pearls have travelled with me through five camps. Hundreds of times I was in situations where I could have lost them, but chance has always helped me out. The shoe with its hidden treasures — my symbol of hope.

In my canteen I have some potato peels. We gathered them yesterday in the garbage pile near the kitchen. We knew that potatoes would be cooked that day, so when we returned from work, we rushed to the kitchen. We found many competitors already sorting through the rubbish, but we were still able to gather some peels before the German cook appeared with his dog and big stick.

Since, as usual, I ate my whole ration of bread in the morning, all my hope now lies in the contents of the canteen. As soon as I can, I seize a few small stones and some branches to make a fire. I add some snow to my canteen and pull a great treasure from my pocket — matches. As the fire starts to burn, I run to the field and pull some weeds, which the French inmates call "pissenlit," *dandelions. I also pull some kind of parsley that Dworzecki likes. The soup is ready soon, and I call Dworzecki. The delicious warmth fills our stomachs.*

A good day today, I say to myself. The work is monotonous, but not too hard, and we are seldom so successful in making a fire and cooking a soup so quickly without being discovered by a guard. I close my eyes, momentarily contented, and become absorbed in my thoughts.

It is a beautiful summer day. My parents have rented a cottage in the country where life is simple and good. The pungent scent of fir and spruce spikes the air. A peasant woman comes every morning with an overflowing basket filled with fruit, white cheeses, and large round loaves of black bread for sale. For lunch, I slice off a large chunk of bread and spread it with cheese. I wash it all down with milk fresh from the cow.

Dworzecki is shaking my arm. I am annoyed. "Oh, Marek! I was dreaming of black bread and milk. Leave me alone."

"Are you crazy? Here, take my shovel, quick. I'll take the mattock."

Another guard is approaching. He pauses not far from us. When he comes closer, Dworzecki takes courage and says to him, "Herr Meister, allow me a question. My friend here is an artist, a "Charaktermaler." *For a piece of bread, he'll draw your picture." No one, including Dworzecki, knows what* "Charaktermaler" *means, but he uses the word because he thinks it makes an impression.*

"I give you the advice to work harder, you scoundrels, or I'll give you a good lesson all right, and it won't be too artistic!"

The Aftermath

In our partnership, Dworzecki plays the role of impresario and I, the artist. I have some skill in drawing, and Dworzecki, like a professional agent, praises me as if I were the second Raphael. The purpose, of course, is to obtain an extra ration of bread. But my reputation in the camp is rather that of a poet. "He is a friend of Tuwim, the famous Polish poet," Dworzecki announces on every possible occasion, although I have never met Tuwim. Dworzecki's eloquent praise appeals to the snobs in the camp — the Polish camp dignitaries, the chief of the hospital, several office workers, and the Blockaelteste Jurek. At the evening distribution of soup Jurek sometimes looks for me in the barrack, yelling: "Where is the poet? Soup for the poet." I share the extra soup with Dworzecki. Ironically, Dworzecki's skill as a physician brings meager returns, while my "poetry" is more substantially rewarded. As strange as it seems in this bestial environment, I am able to touch a sensitive chord with my poems, even in the sadistic Kapos *selected by the Germans for their willingness to oppress fellow inmates.*

In my poems, I try to express the suffering in our lives, and the hope that it will end and we can return home. One poem I write in Polish is about camp inmates forced to stand at attention for several hours. I entitle it, "The Roll Call":

> *"Three times I counted and the counts do not agree.*
> *One son of a bitch is missing.*
> *When I find him, he'll get a lesson,*
> *He and every one in the block."*
>
> *"Form rows, heads to the right.*
> *Stand straight, in columns of five.*
> *Assistants, look in every corner of this block,*
> *On all the beds of boards, and under each one."*
>
> *The chief of the block rages, the assistants search.*

Fear seizes the rows in its claws.
Everybody has already worked ten hours today.
Everybody is hungry, and dead tired.
The roll call may last one hour, or four.
Everybody is weak, some have fainted.
"Kick them aside." One more collapses.
"Let him lie. It does not matter."

All this because the roll call is sacred.
Records, figures and accounts must tally.
Woe, if an error is made,
and the report is incorrect.

Arms stiffen and knees tremble.
These are numbers standing, a nameless human crowd.
"Stand straight, you sons-of-a-bitch,
or woe to your mugs."

They stand, but feel dizzy.
Their eyes become blurred from weariness.
Torn shoes are wet, lice are biting,
And throats are dry with thirst.

They found him at last, under the bunks.
The account finally agrees.
They kicked him, but he was dead.
"The scoundrel won't disturb us any more."

In a distant, burnt out town on the Vistula,
a woman is hugging her child.
"Will Dad return?" "He will, my darling.
I prayed for him the whole night."

But fear and worry,
Despair and misgiving grip her heart.
"Will you return, oh David, my husband?
Will you come back? Will it ever be as it once was?"

Prontosil

"*DON'T MAKE ME ANGRY, you sons of a whore, or you'll die right here.*"
The Lageraelteste, Mundek, *is shouting orders. It is customary in the camp that every second word is a curse; it does not impress anyone. Mundek is a Pole, a country boy. For all his cruelty, he brings a touch of humor to the roll call. His Slavic curses all relate to sex.*

We are standing in five rows of four hundred. Dworzecki and I are side by side. The dignitaries of the camp, the Blockaelteste *and several other functionaries, stand on the right wing.*

Most of us are veterans of several camps and are used to these commands. Dautmergen is the fifth camp in which I've been interned. In Stutthof, the roll call was organized according to the strictest Prussian tradition. The slightest error would entail immediate punishment, even death. The weak and hungry inmates stood ramrod straight and performed the routine precisely and quickly, like automatons. But it was summer at that time in Stutthof, and we stood on dry ground. Now it is fall in Dautmergen, and we are mired in rain and mud. Two inmates have fainted and are being held up on the arms of their neighbors. I do not feel well myself, and I struggle to remain upright.

At the end of the roll call, I faint. It is the first sign of weakness and a warning that I might die of exhaustion. The world fades to black as I fall to the mud. When I open my eyes, I see Dworzecki slapping my face and shouting. "Open your mouth, Henryk! Open your mouth or you'll die!" The sharp slaps bring me back to consciousness, and Dworzecki helps me stand up. I lean on him until the end of the roll call, then he drags me to the hospital door. Engelhart, the Polish doctor, refuses to accept me. "He's a faker, the son-of-a-bitch," he says. "Bring him here when he's about to die." Dworzecki supports me under one arm and someone takes my other. They drag me along just as we dragged Rosenblatt a few months before. An hour later, I feel somewhat better, and the day passes.

The rain continues for days. It attacks our emaciated bodies and chills the marrow of our bones. It is worse than cold and hunger, and death begins to reap its harvest. I tell myself, "I want to live, I will not give up."

Dworzecki and I are working in the canalization group. Our work is to dig deep ditches for pipes which will bring water to the camp from the closest village. Rain makes puddles in the ditches, and we stand in ankle-deep water for ten hours every day burrowing into the earth and removing rocks. Dworzecki's morale is low, and, now, it is my depleted energy that keeps us alive. Despite my fainting episode, I am still an enterprising "organizer" at finding food. My feet have begun to swell worse than ever, and my shoes feel as if they are about to burst. I am having difficulty digging.

One day, I have an unexpected stroke of luck. An SS officer orders me to work in Schoenberg, a small town a few kilometers from our camp. The mayor needs an inter-

preter to assist him in the interrogation of Russian forced laborers. A soldier will take me to and from the village of Schoenberg every day, where I will work in the small city hall.

The job turns out to be a blessing. I am treated well in the mayor's office. A small room is assigned to me in the garret where I can rest between interrogations. The mayor has a large German shepherd. A huge slab of meat is suspended on a hook from the ceiling of the garret. Once in a while, someone climbs the stairs to the garret to cut off a piece of meat for the dog. I am fortunate enough to become dining partners with the dog, and every day I am able to cut off a chunk of meat to bring it back and eat with Dworzecki. My strength is returning.

Three or four German women work in the mayor's office. They are all kind to me. One young widow in particular enjoys talking from time to time. She wants to help me with my swollen feet and says she will speak to her boyfriend, an SS officer who works as a paramedic in the camp. Naturally, this frightens me, but I cannot tell her how unwelcome her offer is. The SS man looks at my feet and advises me to change my shoes. Of course, I cannot part with them, because of the treasure hidden in the hollowed-out sole. "They are quite comfortable," I reply, and hope he will soon forget about me.

A week or so later, a rumor spreads through the camp that half the inmates will be evacuated to Bergen-Belsen. As bad as Dautmergen is, the horror of Bergen-Belsen is far greater. We know how slim our chances of survival would be there.

The rumor proves to be true. One morning at roll call, three SS men, including the paramedic who examined my feet, stroll along the ranks to select the victims to be sent to Bergen-Belsen. When the paramedic sees me, he says,

"Aren't you the man with the swollen feet? Only strong men will remain here. Step forward and join the group for Bergen-Belsen."

Survival in the camps is a matter of miracles. Energy, strength, endurance, and will are only contributing factors. It is a lottery in which only those who win again and again have a chance to survive.

When the Kapos *see that I am being selected for evacuation, they join forces to save the "poet." They argue that the swelling is only a temporary condition and has almost disappeared. The paramedic yields.*

Dworzecki and I are known as notoriously lazy workers and we have to be careful. One day when I am being persecuted by a Kapo, *Dworzecki protests in my defense, and he is beaten badly. The rain has drained his resistance and, by nightime, he is running a high fever. He is admitted to the hospital the following morning and his arm, which has become infected after the beating, is operated on without an anaesthetic. The operation is done under such unhygienic conditions that he, like so many others, contracts a serious blood infection. Only prontosil pills can save him.*

After another week of rain, a terrible wave of death decimates the camp. People die at roll call, while they work, during the night. On the average, one can hardly expect to live longer than a month under such conditions. Most of us have symptoms of exhaustion which the Germans euphemistically call "AKS" for Algemeine Körperschwäche, *general-body-weakness. The few healthy men and the better-fed functionaries of the camp call us "muselmans." There is no pity and no compassion. The ruthless law of the camp equates weakness with death.*

I feel that my turn is near. The hunger and long hours of work in the rain have broken down my resistance. I am alone, my friend in the hospital. If I am going to die, I want to save him before my end. I offer my bread and soup for two or three pills of prontosil, but in spite of my generous offer, no one can provide the little red pills. Then I think of Iserke.

Before the war, Iserke belonged to the Jewish underworld in Vilno called the "Shtarke, *toughs.*" Our friendship began in Estonia where he was the soul of the musical concerts in our camp barracks. On Sunday evenings we would all get down from our "beds," form a circle, and clap as Iserke performed fantastic Cossack dances.

When I tell him of my desperate efforts to get prontosil for my friend, Iserke advises me to join his work group on the following day. They will be working near the French prisoners of war, one of whom, Iserke has noticed, wears a Red-Cross band on his arm.

To change work groups is strictly forbidden, but on the following morning I use my bread ration to bribe the foreman to let me join Iserke's group. Helmut, the Kapo *of that work group, is a tall German with the face of a boxer, but he is one of the few* Kapos *who still harbor some human feelings. Even so, when he sees me in his group, he starts beating me.*

"I will go with you even if you beat me to death," I say.

"You're crazy, you dirty dog."

"I want to save my friend," I plead. "He'll die if I don't bring him some prontosil."

Helmut stops beating me. After a long march, we arrive at the work place, and Helmut calls me over. "Come, you with the face of the suffering Christ. I will show you the way to the Frenchmen."

When I reach the group of French prisoners of war, I approach a man with a Red-Cross band on his arm. "My friend is dying," I say. "I must have prontosil to save him." The Frenchman says he does not have any pills with him, but he promises to do his best to bring some the next day.

Helmut's beating has exhausted me. My chronic dysentery is getting much worse. My feet and hands are like pieces of ice. When I return to work, I have to carry such heavy logs that I fall. I want to stand up, but I cannot. A passing foreman kicks me with his boot. I do not move. In a delirium, I see him spit and hear him say, "This one is ready." A Russian approaches and steals my bread. A Pole takes my canteen. "He does not need it. He is dead, the son-of-a-bitch." The earth is covered with the first frost, and my face rests on the icy ground. I put my hands over my head and think, "Mother, this must be my end. Maybe it is better so, better than if I were to live comfortably some day, knowing that you died and I was not there to defend you, or die with you." I lie on the ground for a long time hallucinating, not feeling the cold. Two faces bend over me. I hear a voice saying in Yiddish, "Look, this is the guy who fought against the Di Ponte brothers in Estonia." They lift me up.

The day's work is finished and the group is ready to return to the camp. When Helmut sees me, he orders Iserke and a few others to drag me along. Still hallucinating the next day, I march to work and, finally, I hold in my hand six red tablets of prontosil. Again, I return to the camp on Iserke's arm, then bring the tablets to Dworzecki.

"These tablets are for you, Marek," I tell him, "but I'm finished. I have no strength left, and I cannot struggle any longer."

Dworzecki weeps. "No," he says, "you must live. You will live."

The following days drift through my mind like visions in a fog. I notice a Belgian physician looking at me and twirling his index finger by his temple to indicate that I am *a lunatic. Dworzecki tells me later that I have a wild look in my eyes and that I give the impression of being crazy. My desire to eat disappears. All I want to do is sleep, to close my eyes and cover my head with a blanket. I am admitted to the* "Schonungsblock," *a branch of the hospital for convalescents. Dworzecki is also admitted there and, under his care, I slowly regain some energy. The will to survive gradually returns.*

By February, of the thousand men in the group with whom I arrived at Dautmergen, only forty remain.

Marek Dworzecki

THE TRAIN RACES THROUGH the northern plains of France. My excitement grows. Perhaps Dworzecki's survival is a sign of yet another miracle. Fate will grant me one more favor, and I will find my wife in France.

I share the train compartment with two young soldiers returning home from the French occupation zone in Germany, and a young woman and older man who are complaining about the hard times. I listen with pleasure to the sound of the French language, which contrasts so much with the heavy guttural tones of German.

"It is so difficult to get potatoes," the woman laments, "and you can forget about meat."

"Yes, it is hard," confirms the old man. "Even the wine is watered."

"We don't worry as long as there are pretty women in Paris," interrupts one of the soldiers. "Here, let me sing you a song." He sings a song that I heard many years ago. I join him in the last refrain.

The soldier is delighted. "How do you know this song?" he inquires.

"I heard it before the war in a French village where I was staying near the border of Spain, between St. Girons and Luchon."

The Aftermath

"St. Girons? That's my home town. I am going there now. How wonderful that you know my country. Have you ever been to the Pic de Montvalier?"

"Yes, I have. And to the summer masquerade balls in St. Girons. Young people from all the neighboring villages used to come there."

This conversation brings back a flood of memories of my student years in France before the war.

I am picking grapes in a vineyard on the slope of a mountain. Heavy clusters hang from the branches. Cows graze close by. I am twenty years old, spending my vacation in the Pyrenées. Next to me is a young herdswoman, Delphine. She is nineteen, with brown eyes and a pretty, delicate face. She is wearing a ribbon bound around her head with a big cockade, and is holding a long stick for the cows. She looks as if she had stepped out of a painting by Fragonard.

"Listen," Delphine says, "I have decided to go to Paris. I cannot live with my step-mother any longer. My sister is a seamstress in Paris and she'll help me get a job. Why don't you come with me?"

"What will your step-mother say, Delphine?"

"She will be only too glad. And nothing will stop me anyway."

In two days, we are in Paris. We meet Delphine's sister, who promises to find her work as a seamstress. In the meantime, we spend the days en flânant, *strolling along the streets of Paris.*

Delphine is fascinated by the beautiful fashions displayed in the windows on rue St. Honoré or worn by the chic women promenading on the Champs Elysées. After a few weeks she catches on to many of the secrets of Parisian elegance, and I watch amazed at the metamorphosis of a Cinderella becoming a lady before my eyes. Was this the same person I had known in the village?

I learn to appreciate French art and culture, and the French language — an admirable tool for expressing oneself with clarity. Wanting to learn more, I spend long hours at the Ste. Geneviève library. Displeased, Delphine tries to tear me away.

"Enough reading," she grumbles. "Come, you promised we'd go to the Casino de Paris."

That time of innocence seems so long ago, and I hardly recognize the naive young man I was then. Now I am returning to Paris to search for my wife and to meet Dworzecki, my companion in suffering. Who knows whatever happened to sweet Delphine?

The train slows down and finally stops at the Gare de L'Est. I inhale the once familiar scents of Paris.

From the station I take the *métro* to St. Michel, then walk to the rue des Ecoles, passing some students, workers, and young couples holding each other close. In my pocket is Marek Dworzecki's address. I enter the hotel. The *concierge,* a fat, older woman, is relaxing with her morning coffee. Two big cats sit on the counter next to her. She directs me to Dworzecki's room. I climb six flights up a narrow staircase and knock.

The door opens, and there stands my friend. He has gained some weight and his hair has grown back, but he has the same deep-set, sad eyes peering from beneath his dark, commanding eyebrows. He recognizes me, and his face lights up.

"Henryk? Can it be true?" We embrace. He pushes me back to look at me. He just shakes his head, smiling. "I never stopped thinking of you, hoping you survived. What a joy to see you, Henryk."

"And I discovered only recently that you are alive, Marek, thank God. I read your article in the newspaper. It was just as though you were talking to me. And now to see you! The food of Paris has done you good, I see. You look wonderful."

"But Henryk, why did it take you so long to come to Paris? Did you forget our promise to meet here, if we survived?"

"No, I didn't forget, Marek, believe me. But I have been searching throughout Europe for Lydia. Have you by any chance heard anything about her?" I doubt that he has, but I ask this question of every survivor I meet.

"I know a couple of young women here who were in the same camp with her. They escaped, and told me that she did too."

My heart leaps. "Is she here? Is Lydia in Paris?"

"No. They don't know where she is. All they know is that she escaped on the day of the evacuation."

"I already know that. But all my efforts to find her have failed. I know she tried to escape, but sometimes I fear that she was killed just before the liberation."

"Nonsense! I'll take you right away to meet the women who know her."

I am so overwhelmed that I almost forget to ask about my friend's loved ones. "Marek, I'm afraid to ask you. I know that your wife Miriam was in the camp of Kloga, in Estonia. Did she escape? Is she alive?"

He bows his head. He does not reply. I remain silent, knowing that nothing I could say would help.

Finally, he answers. "No. I have no hope anymore. I know she did not survive."

Another silence.

"And your sister?"

"My sister was killed there, too. They were both in the same camp, Kloga." He sighs, then tells the rest of the story in a dead, flat voice. "A few days before the Russians came, the inmates of the camp, some fifteen hundred people, mostly women, were all killed. The camp was in a forest. After the roll-call, they were ordered to gather logs from the woods. A group of a few hundred were ordered to throw the logs into a long deep ditch, then forced to lie on them, face down. They were shot with machine guns. A second group of people were forced to place logs on the corpses and to lie on the logs. They were shot, too. Everything very methodical, making the victims create their own massive funeral pyre. The Germans massacred row after row. Then they poured gasoline on the bodies, and set them aflame. Only ninety out of the fifteen hundred people somehow survived to tell what happened. My wife and sister were not among them."

Dworzecki stops speaking and turns his face aside. He is silently sobbing, his entire body shaking.

After a few minutes, he composes himself and continues.

"When the Russians came, they found the place of the massacre. Pictures were taken and even published. I have seen some of them."

I cannot utter a word.

"I am alone. I try to find oblivion in work, in my writing. I don't practice medicine because I have such an urge to write. I am the associate editor of a magazine here in Paris."

I look around. It is a typical, modest Parisian hotel room with a view of the roofs of Paris. Papers and books are spread all around, on the chest of drawers, on the bed, in the corners of the room. On the table, there is a bottle of wine and a croissant in the middle of another pile of papers. I hear the rustle of mice scurrying in the chest.

"I see you haven't changed," I try to joke to relieve the tension. "You are as untidy today as you were in the camps."

"Oh, yes. This is a fault of mine and it gives me a lot of trouble. Only yesterday I went to a restaurant not far from here. After dinner, I realized that I had left my wallet in my room. I explained this to the waiter and told him that I would return with the money. I was already on the sixth floor, ready to open the door, when I realized that I left the key to my room on the table in the restaurant."

We both laugh, feigning good humor.

Dworzecki dresses. We go down for a quick breakfast in a coffeehouse at the corner. Half an hour later, we are climbing the staircase of a small, dusty hotel near the church of Sacré-Coeur. A young woman opens the door. Dworzecki introduces me as Lydia's husband.

"Oh yes," she says. "Lydia and I were together in Magdeburg. I admired her because of her courage. I was with her when she saved a friend's mother during a selection. A German soldier was ready to send the older woman to death. Her daughter was absolutely frozen with terror. Lydia jumped in, pretending that the older woman was her own mother, and somehow convinced the soldier that 'her mother' was quite fit to work.

"We always stayed close in the camp, but we were separated on the day of the evacuation. I managed to hide in a canteen for French workers, not far from the factory. There I heard that Lydia was taken on the forced march from the camp. She was with another friend, Delores Valdés, from Marseilles."

Marseilles

IT IS A CRISP AUTUMN DAY and the sun is shining brightly as the train pulls into Marseilles. I walk quickly from the railway station to the Prefecture. All I know is the name Dolores Valdés. I plan to look for her as soon as I obtain her address from the Prefecture. The office is closed for a lunch recess.

I walk on the lively Canebière, the main street of Marseilles, past cafés, stores and street vendors. People appear happy. Life goes on all around. What motivates these people, I wonder. What are they after? For me the flow of life has come to a standstill.

I come to a harbor where several ships are docked. A big anchor has been thrown in front of some planks. A few workers in dark shirts and broad velvet trousers sit nearby on the planks, eating soup and bread. I lie down not far from them, folding my coat under my head.

I want to forget for awhile my despair, my stolen youth, my broken life, the hopelessness I face. I gaze up at the blue, cloudless sky.

Nearby, one of the workers, an Italian, begins singing plaintively. His voice is sweet. The melody of the song mingles with the rush of the waves as they wash against the stony walls of the pier.

I return to the Prefecture. It is still closed. Not far away, I notice a building with a plaque on the wall that reads, *"Maison des Deportés."* Inside, I ask for the address of Dolores Valdés who, I explain, was deported, and who, I believe, has recently returned to Marseilles.

A girl searches for the address. "Yes, I have it. Dolores Valdés lives with her parents in Julienne, a suburb of Marseilles. Here is the address. You can get there by streetcar in an hour."

The streetcar runs along the harbor. We pass ships, docks, workshops, then still more ships. At last we reach a suburb inhabited mostly by Spaniards. Passers-by show me the way. I come to a ramshackle, single-story house. I enter and find an old man and woman sitting at a table.

"Buenas noches. I have come to see Miss Dolores Valdés," I say. "She was in a labor camp with my wife, Lydia. Did she ever tell you anything about my wife? Do you know where Lydia is?" The old people look at me quizzically, and I realize they may be somewhat hard of hearing. I repeat myself more loudly. "Sit down, *señor,"* says the old man kindly. "Is your wife's name Lydia by any chance?" I eagerly answer that it is. "Ah, yes, she has mentioned that name many times. Our daughter will come back soon, and she will speak with you." It seems like hours before I hear footsteps on the gravel outside. A pretty young woman enters the room. She has olive skin, shining black eyes, and raven hair, a quintessential Spanish *señorita.*

"Dolores, this is the husband of the girl you told us about," the old man says in Spanish. "Oh, you are Lydia's husband!" she exclaims. "You are looking for her?" I nod, and she puts her hand on my arm. "Please, try not to worry. I know that if anyone could have survived, it would be Lydia. But I cannot tell you where she is. We were separated on the day of the evacuation."

My heart sinks. I again despair that I will ever find my wife. "I was told that you escaped together. That's why I'm here — to find out what happened."

"We were together. Lydia and I and two Polish girls in our group. We ran from the march at the same time, but the other two went in a different direction. The last time I saw Lydia, she was running down a narrow side street, dodging through piles of rubbish. I was afraid to follow her. I hid in a ruin. It was cold, and I was very scared. There were bombs dropping overhead all night. The next morning, the Americans came in and occupied the part of the town where I hid."

"Did you hear anything about my wife later?"

"No. There was so much confusion on the first few days after liberation. And after a week, I left for France. But I have kept the piece of paper with Lydia's address which she gave me when we were still in the camp."

She crosses the room and takes a piece of paper from a drawer. "Here it is," she says, handing it to me.

I read my wife's name and the address where she lived in Warsaw with her parents. Lydia wrote this with her own hand, I think, holding the piece of paper. This may be the only thing of her that remains.

I have many questions that I urgently want to ask, but my desire to leave is even stronger. I want to be alone or, at least, among people who are not aware of my anguish.

"Thank you," I say to Dolores, "I must go now," as I move to the door.

"Won't you share our modest meal, *señor?*" the old woman asks.

"No, *gracias*. I must go. I wish you the best."

Dolores is deeply moved. "I will walk with you to the streetcar," she insists.

"No, please. I thank you, but I'd rather you didn't. I hope you understand, but I need to be alone. *Adios.*"

"*Adios señor,* and may *Dios* give you back your wife."

The night is stifling. I walk in the direction of the streetcar station but can't find it. I stop in front of a bar. A phonograph is playing: *"Besame, besame mucho."* There is no door, just strings of red, blue and mauve beads hanging in the entrance, as in an Oriental bazaar.

I go in. A tall, black American GI stands in front of the bar, muttering to himself. Next to him, a handsome French sailor slouches over, staring morosely into an empty glass. A girl sits on a stool between them. Her face is pretty, but worn. Her lips are painted bright red, her eyelids blue. She crosses her shapely legs, revealing a rose garter with a cockade under her short skirt. All three are drunk. The GI continues to mutter. The girl laughs and hiccups at the same time.

"Give me a Calvados," I say to the stooped old woman sitting behind the bar.

The four people watch me while I drink.

"You seem to be so sad," says the girl in a husky voice. "I will console you."

I order two more Calvados and hand one to the girl. She stands up, puts one arm around my neck and plays with my necktie. "You're a real darling," she tells me. I feel her breath on my neck and smell the strong scent of alcohol and cigarettes. Her breast is pressed against my arm. *"Plaisir d'amour ne dure qu'un moment,"* the sailor sings, swaying on his stool. *"Chagrin d'amour dure toute la vie."*

Why not? I ponder as I drink. Why not go to a back room with this sweet, young whore? She is lonely. I am lonely. I am only fooling myself, hoping to find my wife. *Plaisir d'amour.* Perhaps that's all there is, after all.

I suddenly feel repelled by my thoughts. But I do not have anything against the girl, or these people. I empty my glass and pay for the drinks. Someone shows me the way to the streetcar.

Back in Marseilles, I walk the streets aimlessly. I find myself at the harbor again, standing in the same place I was at noon.

I lie down on some planks. From far away comes the shrill sound of a ship's siren. I try to stand up, but my head spins, and I lie down again, looking up into the night sky.

Faces appear before my eyes. The girl from the bar is laughing, "I want to console you, darling." The black soldier stammers something unintelligible. The old woman fills the glasses, over and over again. Hitler's face emerges from the darkness. He is yelling, *"Als ich vor zwanzig Jahren als unbekannter Soldat....* When I was an unknown soldier twenty years ago...." The Italian worker sings, *"Ti amo e non può vivere senza di te."*

Zionism

"ONLY ONE THING can save you from despair," Dworzecki tells me when I arrive back in Paris. "I have an ideal that gives meaning to my life."

"What is that?" I ask.

"We spoke of it many times in the camps when we did not know whether we would survive. It has been the hope of so many generations, and now our generation can achieve it, at last."

"You mean Palestine?"

"Yes, Zion."

Dworzecki opens the Bible that lies on the table and reads from the pages of Isaiah:

"For the Lord shall comfort Zion: He will comfort all her waste places and he will make her wilderness like Eden, and her desert like the garden of the Lord; joy and gladness shall be found therein, thanksgiving, and the voice of melody."

There is great dignity in these words. My friend continues:

"Look upon Zion, the city of our solemnities: thine eyes shall see Jerusalem a quiet habitation, a tabernacle that shall not be taken down."

His voice trembles with emotion.

"And the ransomed of the Lord shall return and come to Zion with songs and everlasting joy upon their heads: they shall obtain joy and gladness, and sorrow and sighing shall flee away."

He closes the book.

"Look, Henryk," he says, "I married Zion. I loved my wife and my parents, but I love Zion even more. I would sacrifice my heart and my body for Zion. There is only one thing on my mind: Zion."

In his excitement, he stands up and paces the room.

"I am a Jew and I want to live like one. When the Teutons were running half-naked in forests, we already had the Bible, the Prophets, and the *Song of Songs*. I do not want to be a tenant in foreign houses any longer. I want to be at home at last, even if my home is small and poor. I prefer to live in a place that is my own, where I can do what I want, than to live where I must depend on a landlord's whims. I want to give all of my strength to Zion. I no longer practice medicine, although I loved my work, because as a journalist I can serve Zion better. When my father was dying, I promised him that I would live in Palestine. Look, Henryk, you are my only true friend. Promise me that you will do the same."

"I am a Jew," I reply, "and I cannot afford to act independently of that fact, since the outside world exerts so much pressure on every Jew. Yet I must tell you that I am against inflated nationalism and religious fanaticism. They have been the root of sufferings over the ages. The ancient Greeks considered all foreigners to be barbarians. The Arabs regard themselves as the noblest nation. The Chinese think they are the only civilized people. The French reminisce about their glory under Napoleon. The British are convinced of their colonial mandate. The German 'master race' looks down on all others. *Deutschland Über Alles.*"

"And every nation wants to monopolize God. Even we Jews consider ourselves the Chosen People. What is the result of such attitudes? Patriotic euphoria, the urge to conquer and dominate, false heroism, Nazi madness. What is nationalism but egoism of the masses? I have always believed that the progress of humankind lies in subduing nationalistic tendencies all over the world."

"But your words are a luxury that Jews cannot afford," Dworzecki answers. "All peoples in the world have a home, some better, some worse, but their own. Only the Jews are outside. We cannot think of abolishing our nationalism until we have a safe place, too. We must put an end to our homelessness. We need a place under the sun. Zion is the small piece of desert that we want to transform into a garden with the sweat of our brows. If it is refused to us, we must fight to win it, or die fighting."

I decide to stay in Paris, sharing Dworzecki's room. He spends his time writing, and he is often invited to give lectures. He is well known and respected in many circles in France and other countries.

One day Dworzecki receives an invitation to give a lecture in Brussels and is gone for several days. When I welcome him back at the railroad station, he shows me a painting he has brought back with him. I cannot keep my eyes off it. The painting portrays a group of refugees. Their dark eyes reveal a profound sadness and anxiety. It seems that their suffering lips could tell endless stories of persecution.

"Marek, this is an unusual painting," I remark. "The artist must have been in a feverish trance. How did you get it?"

Dworzecki tells me the story of how he obtained the painting. At a ceremony in his honor at the Sorbonne, he met the Belgian editor of a Catholic newspaper. When Dworzecki was in Brussels, the editor invited him to dine with him and his wife in their home. She was a charming woman, and the conversation was delightful. After dinner, the editor was called away by an urgent message from his newspaper. While his wife and Dworzecki were waiting for his return, Dworzecki admired the excellent collection of paintings on the walls of the living room. He was particularly struck by one small painting which evoked his own painful memories.

"Who painted this?" he asked.

"Why, I did," she replied.

Dworzecki reflected for a moment and was convinced that his instinct did not mislead him. "Madame," he said, "you are Jewish."

Her face flushed and she looked distraught.

"Please, Madame, only a Jewish person could paint like this."

After a few moments, she confessed that it was true, she was Jewish, but that her husband did not know. He was a deeply religious Catholic who had saved her life. Before her parents died, they managed to leave her in the protection of nuns. Then, when the convent was being evacuated, he took her in. They soon fell in love and married. But for all these years, even after the war, she never told him her secret.

Dworzecki, sure of her husband's character, tried to convince her to reveal the truth. Finally she agreed to let Dworzecki speak to him on her behalf. Her husband was taken aback by the news, but Dworzecki's judgment of his character proved correct.

"I cannot describe to you, Henryk," Dworzecki continues, "my pleasure at seeing the love and harmony which bound them. As I was leaving, the young woman took the painting from the wall and gave it to me. 'Take it with you, Doctor,' she said, 'and when you look at it, think of what you have done for me.'"

I am very impressed by Dworzecki's strong convictions and think about them often over the next few weeks. What a special man Marek is, I think. His commitment to Zionism gives meaning to his life. The Jews have to build a homeland, that much is clear after what we have been through. But I am not sure how much I can offer, or what my part would be.

Dworzecki feels that I have a talent for diplomacy and that I could find fulfilment in political service. He introduces me to a number of prominent Zionist leaders. I meet Rubashov* and we discuss my prospective assignment as an ambassador. I speak with Yarblum, head of Jewish-French organizations, and spend an evening with Ruth Kliger, Chief of the Jewish agency in Paris.

The most memorable meeting is with Ben Gurion in his room at the California Hotel, near the Champs Elysées. He speaks in a thin, high voice, but his strong, square face and piercing gaze reveal his exceptional determination and strength. "Ben Gurion thinks," Dworzecki tells me later, "that you should start as an aide to Chertok, the man in charge of foreign relations. He said that he would arrange for you to meet Chertok in Paris."

As exciting as it is to meet these great leaders, I find that I cannot really think about Palestine. I am obsessed by my search for Lydia. I try to find distractions in the charms of Paris. I visit the places I loved in my student years: the steep streets of Montmartre, the *bouquinistes* on the Quais,

---

* Editors's note: Rubashov later becomes the president of Israel under his adopted Hebrew name, Shazar.

the pond in the Tuileries where children sail their little ships, the fountain in the Luxembourg Garden where couples in love stroll arm in arm.

But neither the charms of Paris nor the cause of Zionism can change my preoccupation. Every pair of lovers embracing in the street reminds me of my loneliness. I envy Dworzecki — he has found a passion, a reason to live. I do not want to disappoint my closest friend, perhaps my only friend left alive. But I know that I cannot devote myself to Zionism, as he has done, to the exclusion of everything else.

After another week of rumination, I finally tell Dworzecki: "I must disappoint you, my friend. I cannot take the path you wish. I must go back to Germany, although I hate returning there. I don't know if I will find Lydia, but if there is still a chance, it can only be there at the crossroads of all displaced persons. I am leaving for Munich tomorrow."

I sleep fitfully, unhappy to be leaving my best friend again. I am in conflict about returning to Germany, but know that I must continue my search for Lydia.

The Germans

WINTER HAS COME to Munich. The wind howls through the ruins of houses, whistles through the holes that were once doors and windows, and sweeps dry leaves over heaps of rubble. People's faces are grim, without smiles or warmth, as grim as the autumn skies above. Everything around me looks ugly and hopeless. I remember my life before the war like a painting in beautiful, bright colors. The war has smeared all the colors into this grey blur. I feel the weight of my loneliness. I want to talk with a friend, but can only talk to myself.

Sonya, a young survivor with whom I work at the American Joint Distribution Committee, probably senses my loneliness. She invites me to dinner to meet her husband Geniek. I feel an immediate affinity with him. He is handsome, with a dark olive complexion, and sad, brooding eyes. I try to be a cheerful dinner companion. We chat about old friends from before the war, and I discover that Geniek knew my beautiful second cousin Danka quite well. I am thrilled. "You know Danka? She is my favorite cousin, and such a fine artist! Do you know what happened to her?"

Geniek looks down into his plate. Sonya gets up abruptly, saying she must attend to something in the kitchen. Geniek finally looks at me. "This will not be easy for you to hear, Henryk, but you should know. Danka is dead. I witnessed her death. I will never forget the scene as long as I live. Do you really want to hear?"

"Yes," I tell him. "Of course, I assumed she must be dead, but I wasn't sure. She was so beautiful, so gifted. Tell me, Geniek."

"All right," he sighs. "This was during the last days of the Warsaw Uprising, when the entire ghetto was in flames. The streets were covered with rubble, broken furniture, overturned carts. A stench rose from the corpses. The billowing smoke and suffocating heat from the houses turned that afternoon into a replica of hell. My wife and children had already been killed. I was hiding in a nest of a ruined upperfloor apartment along with Danka, her brother Mietek, a couple with a nine-year-old girl, and a few others. A wall of the apartment had collapsed, so the nest was visible from the street to the passing Germans. I decided to walk across a plank to an adjacent building, and told them to follow if I made it.

"The plank was a narrow rafter that had fallen and lodged itself next to the remains of a brick wall. I didn't look down as I inched along, trying to find handholds in the bricks where the mortar had crumbled. A spider ran out of a crevice onto my hand. In that frozen moment, I realized that the spider could hide, but I couldn't. As if to mock me, it spun a thin filament into the wind, and let itself be borne away.

"Finally, I reached the other side and collapsed on a pile of rubble. I was sweating, starving, half out of my mind. I composed myself and waved to the others to follow. But they wouldn't do it. They were too frightened, or too tired. I heard machine gun fire, then the thud of boots. I hid behind the rubble, but I could still see Danka lying with her head on her brother's lap.

"I heard the familiar Nazi scream, *'Schweinehunde! Saujuden! Alles runter! Schnell!* Swine! Pigs! Everyone down! Fast!' Horrified, I saw Danka, Mietek and the others descend the shaky staircase to the courtyard below, where they were forced to face a wall. It all happened very quickly. I heard a burst of machine gun fire. I saw their bodies fall to the ground. I watched the blood form a pool around them. And I could do nothing, nothing. I could only crouch there like a rat in the rubble, not making a sound."

Geniek stops talking. He looks at me, shaking his head. "Henryk, I am so sorry. I wish it could be otherwise. Oh, God. I wish so many things could be otherwise." I reach over the table and touch his hand. We sit there in silence.

Finally, I make a lame excuse and leave.

In the streetcars I rub shoulders with the German people. Murderers! Look at the one in the corner with the scar on his face. I imagine him in an SS uniform. He certainly raised his arm and shouted *"Heil Hitler!"* At his morning coffee, he would read in the papers: "Our troops enter Warsaw," or "Kiev is taken." Perhaps he was a high-ranking Nazi. He stole furniture in France, paintings in Holland, and brought a silver-fox coat from Norway for his wife. He drank champagne from Epernay and ate caviar from Crimea. He smelled the smoke of people being turned into ash in the crematoria.

Two girls chat next to me in the streetcar. They have healthy, chubby faces, big bosoms and broad hips. "Hans kissed me yesterday," one whispers to the other. Danka is dead, I think, and Lydia may have been murdered, too, and these girls are chatting and laughing. Hans is probably a murderer, too. Perhaps he hung people in a concentration camp, or shot them in the back of their heads. Tomorrow he will kiss this girl who is healthy as a cow, and soon she will bring another little Hans into the world. I can no longer tolerate the girls' laughter and get off the streetcar.

I hate them. I hate them all. What can I do? I wish I were a flier and could drop bombs on Germany, to see the flames below me and know that they spread destruction and death.

Am I going crazy? I ask myself. This is madness. Are all Germans guilty of Germany's crimes? And even if so many of them are murderers, have I the right to be a murderer too?

I remember some cases of humane behavior on the part of the Germans, but they were so rare amid the overwhelming cruelty. What about those who looked on in silence? If I am on a streetcar and see someone being strangled, I ask myself, would I not try to save the victim? Could I just watch and do nothing? The guilt of the German people lies not only with the perpetrators, but with the silence of the onlookers. Their silence made the crimes possible.

I wander into a movie house. The film, *Die Todesmuehlen,* The Mills of Death, depicts the horrors of the concentration camps. Ghastly faces appear on the screen, heaps of corpses, piles of gold fillings extracted from the mouths of victims, stacks of dolls taken away from children before their death. I study the faces in the audience. They do not seem impressed by the scenes they are watching. I cannot stand their indifference, and I leave the theater.

How good it would be not to feel hate, to have peace in one's heart, to believe in God and justice and humanity. But how can one believe in humanity after having seen the evil of which man is capable? Humanity. A ridiculous word corrupted by politicians. "War is a natural state," I once read in a military encyclopedia, "interrupted by intervals that serve as the preparation for war. War is a reflection of the laws of nature." Yet animals in the jungle do not kill for sport, revenge or ideology. Why do some people have so much power over millions of others? What gives any man the right to say to another, "I am superior to you. I will make the decisions about your slavery or freedom, your life or death." I think about Beethoven's words: "There is only one superiority, the superiority of a good heart."

One day Major Ordway, my protector, tells me he is being recalled to the States. Before leaving, he wants to help me further. He asks what kind of work I would like to do. "You are an engineer. Are you interested in managing a factory?"

"No, Major. For a few months I will not work at all. I cannot concentrate."

"Well, that's all right. But you must not lose hope of finding your wife. And before I leave, I want to help you get a nice apartment."

I am assigned a cozy apartment with a garden in Nymphenburg, a quiet and elegant area of Munich. The windows face a tree-lined avenue that runs along a canal. From the window I can see the placid water and watch the changing colors of the leaves.

The days pass, lonely and dreary. Everything seems empty and meaningless. Leo, my young Polish friend, is my driver. It feels strange to have a chauffeur, but I enjoy his company. Leo becomes quite attached to me, and considers me his mentor. "You will see," he says. "One day I will take you and your wife for a pleasure drive around town."

"Ah, Leo. Miracles happen only in fairy tales."

I live through days of despair.

The survivors' efforts to find their family and friends are beginning to slow down. Some have found each other, but the majority have already learned the terrible fate of their loved ones. Scenes of reunions become rare. The problem facing the survivors now is how to begin their lives again. Organizations extend some help. New temporary camps for refugees are set up.

The offices of the Jewish Committee and the office of the American Joint Distribution Committee in Munich move to a building on Siebertstrasse. Along with the Army and UNRRA, these organizations provide food, clothing, and roofs over the heads of the survivors. But their help is only temporary. What survivors want most is to get out of Germany, out of Europe, and to rebuild their lives in Palestine or overseas. The war with Japan is over, the UN has come into being, and the nightmare of the atom bomb now hovers over the world. Chaos still reigns all around.

For too many, waiting still means grey barracks and camp routines, listening to the sounds of the German language, continuing their existence as bystanders to life. But there is hope that this will soon be over, and new life can begin. Only a little more patience. Many people live through anguish similar to mine. When I ask a survivor if his wife is alive, he doesn't answer, only sighs as if to say, "Why did it happen? Why is fate so cruel?"

But the eternal law of regeneration begins to assert itself. Young survivors find love with one another, and those who have lost their spouses find new ones. "I would have gone crazy if I had not married again," one honest man tells me. "I couldn't stand the loneliness, the memories of the past." Another confides, "In my mind, the image of my dead wife has become mixed with the woman I just married. They are becoming the same person to me. Is that a betrayal?" I assure him that it is probably a normal process. It is the way humans cope with loss, I think. I do not tell him about Lydia. It seems that everywhere I look among the refugees, women's bellies bloom with the weight of a new generation. You would think that they would hesitate to bring new life into such a world, but I realize that this fertility is a sign of health. I only wish I shared in their renewed optimism.

I get a dog, a beautiful, black spaniel, six months old, whom I name Johnny. I grow very attached to him. In the morning Johnny comes to the edge of my bed to find out if I am still asleep. He waits until I open my eyes and speak to him. Then he springs onto the bed, full of joy. Every day we take long walks so he can run and chase after squirrels. In the evenings he lies next to my chair, watching me with his big, faithful eyes.

I live with memories. The present mixes with the past, which I can see with astonishing clarity. I am in the streets of Warsaw, the narrow lanes of the Vilno ghetto, the barracks of the concentration camp in Germany.

The Letter

WINTER HAS COME to Munich. Hopeless days drag on, one after another. I ask Leo to go to the Committee on Siebertstrasse to see if there is any correspondence for me. It is a very cold January night. Wood burns in the stove. The room is dark but for the light cast by the flames. I sprawl on the sofa, staring at the ceiling. Johnny lies nearby. If I had to go through the hell of the concentration camps, I ask myself, but with the hope of seeing Lydia again, would I choose to do so? Yes, I whisper aloud.

I begin to hum a Russian song: "*Me prosteemsya s toboy oo poroga, I byt moshet navsyegdah.* We shall separate at the threshold, perhaps forever." I feel utterly lonely.

The door bell rings abruptly. Johnny starts barking. I open the door.

Leo stands there, holding a letter in his hand. He looks very excited. Without a word, he hands the letter to me.

United

IT IS FIVE O'CLOCK in the morning. The night is cold and so foggy that I cannot see beyond a few meters. My car is parked in front of the house. I am wearing a warm sheepskin coat, fur gloves and felt shoes, all borrowed from Leo.

"Is everything ready?" I ask.

"Yes," Leo answers. "You have a new battery and a spare tire." Even though Leo is supposed to be my driver, I insist on taking this trip alone. I do not want to share the experience with anyone.

The big tree in front of the house has a hole in it. I pull out a piece of paper from my notebook and write, "Welcome home." I put the note into the hole, and cover it with a stone. "I hope the wind won't blow it away," I say before bidding Leo good-bye.

I start the car. The headlights project through a milky haze. I drive fast at first, but I have to slow down. It is like driving through cotton. In the fog the lights illuminate the road for only a short distance ahead. By dawn I reach the Autobahn to Nuremberg. A coat of frost covers the windshield. I have to stop the car every few kilometers to wipe the window.

The day breaks dull and grey, but to me life is shining with all the colors of the rainbow. I stop the car and take the letter from my pocket. I read it for the hundredth time:

To the Tracing Office, Siebertstrasse, Munich:

I have obtained today your address from the Committee in Bergen-Belsen, together with the information that my husband is alive in Munich. Please inform him where I am, and that I am well after a long illness. I am employed by the UNRRA team at the Trilke factory in Hildesheim, near Hanover, in the British zone. Please ask my husband to come to me immediately or, if this is not possible, please telegraph me and I will come to him.

Lydia Turkus Lilienheim

I put the letter, which I know by heart, back into my pocket. I take an exit off the Autobahn and enter Nuremberg. I drive along the ruined streets and past the court building where the war criminals were tried. From afar, I see the long passage that leads from the prison to the court.

The fog lifts as I approach the highway, and I press down on the accelerator. I pass the ruins of Wurzburg and continue northwest toward Frankfurt. By the time I reach Marburg, it has begun to snow, and soon a thick layer covers the windshield. I continue scraping the windshield every few kilometers. Night falls, and I turn on the lights. Flakes of snow dance in their glow.

A sign appears. "You are in the British zone." There is no one at the checkpoint, probably because of the snowstorm. At dawn I pass Goettingen, not far from Hanover. I turn east toward Hildesheim.

The Aftermath

I remember the way. On my first search for Lydia in Germany, I passed through a hundred towns and detours, including this one to Hildesheim. I stopped here, but nobody I asked knew anything about my wife. Now, six months later, I am on the same highway. There will be a long serpentine in awhile, I recall, then a forest and a hill.

Is this real, I wonder, or will I soon wake up from a dream? Is it really possible that Lydia will be waiting for me? I realize that my hands on the steering wheel are shaking. After all this time apart, after all the suffering and heartache, has our love survived along with our battered bodies? Will she still want to be with me? Our life before the war now seems like a fantasy, a closed storybook impossible to open again.

As I enter Hildesheim in the early hours of the morning, the streets of the ruined town are still deserted. I see a German policeman standing at a crossroads.

"Is this the way to the Trilke Werke?" I ask.

"Yes. Follow the trolley bus wires."

After a few minutes, I stop in front of a heavy iron gate. The sign reads: "Trilke Werke. UNRRA Team."

I walk in. A young woman is leaning over some correspondence. "Excuse me," I ask, "does Lydia Lilienheim work here?"

The woman looks up at me, startled. Oh God! It is Lydia. Everything seems to move slowly now. She gets up. "Henyu, is it really you?" She is crying and laughing, "Oh my God, oh my God," as she moves around the desk. I blurt out something, but I don't know what. She appears incredibly radiant, an angel from another world dressed in an U.N. uniform. She is more beautiful than I remember. I notice a slight limp, and then we are together.

We hold one another a long time.

"It's better if you leave this heavy trunk full of books," I tell Lydia. "The car is already overloaded."

"You must be joking, Henyu. I need these books."

"But I'm afraid they are too heavy for the tires. We have to drive some five hundred kilometers to Munich. Do you know how hard it is to change a tire in the middle of winter? If you care so much for these books, there are a lot of other things you could leave behind. This big ugly lamp, for instance."

"Oh no, please. It's not ugly, and it stood on the table near my bed the whole time I was sick."

"Well, what about all these pots and pans? Are you planning to open a hardware store in Munich?"

"You know nothing about housekeeping. You are so used to a bachelor's life; you don't remember what a household requires. Don't worry. We won't have any trouble on the road because my mascot will protect us." She holds up a pillow in the shape of a black cat. "It brought me luck when I was sick."

"But..."

"Please, stop arguing. Why do you argue? Do you enjoy it?"

I stop and realize how silly this is. What difference does any of it make now? Why argue over trivial things when we are alive, and together?

"Yes, Lydia, I love to argue with you. I missed it badly for such a long time. I hope to argue with you many more times!"

"Me too," she answers, the winner of our first quarrel. "Many, many times."

We leave Hildesheim in the afternoon and get on the Autobahn to Munich. The car is so weighed down that we feel every bump. Lydia finally agrees that we have to leave a few things — first some pots, and then, with regret, several books.

On the way, we share stories of what we have been through since the day of our separation in Vilno, nearly three years before. We talk all the way from Hildesheim to Fulda. At one stop along the way, I pull the small box I have been saving out of my pocket, and give it to Lydia. I explain that it is something I bought from Olek, another survivor, with the hope of giving it to her some day.

Lydia takes out the ring, and slips it on her finger. "It looks beautiful on your hand," I tell her. Then I remember the pearls. "But this in not the gift I most wanted to give you." As we drive on, I tell her about the pearls, and about how I had dreamt so often of the day I would place them around her neck. So many times I had been in danger of losing them, and so many times I managed to keep them with me.

My luck forsook me in February, 1945, just two months before the end of the war. The Germans were making a selection for evacuation from Dautmergen. I was "selected" and my group was taken directly from roll call to a barracks surrounded by the SS. There we were ordered to undress and leave our things outside in a pile. Later, we were ordered to pick clothes and shoes from other piles, and board a train to Dachau. Everything happened so quickly that there was no time to act. The cherished pearls that had accompanied my every step through several camps for eighteen long months were lost forever.

"Don't worry about the pearls, Henyu," Lydia tells me, giving me a gentle hug. "We have been far luckier than either of us could have dared to hope." And she tells me the story of her survival in the camps.

Lydia's Story

"WHEN WE WERE SEPARATED in Vilno, Henyu, they put all the women in one corner outside. You remember how miserable and cold it was. They took all the men away. Then they separated children, younger women and older women. Even among the young women, if someone was handicapped or ugly, they didn't like it. They just wanted good-looking, strong young women, who could work.

"I was there when your sister Edwarda refused to part with her Misia. It was the most horrible thing I have ever experienced. We were begging these Germans to leave this little girl. Eight years old, she was not so small. She could have maybe helped in the kitchens. But the German officer would not hear it. He slapped Eda and pushed her and Misia away. I never saw them again.

"It was not just this one officer. They were all shouting and had machine guns. To me, they were all ugly-faced monsters. Inhuman. I kept thinking, Why? Why? Why? Why? I didn't do anything bad. I was a good human being. I was practically a child — well, not a child, but so young! All I had done so far in my life was go to school and try to be honest. And my parents were good people. Very, very good people. I just didn't understand why it happened.

"So we were separated. Later we found out that all the older women and children were killed. The rest of us were taken to a labor camp in Latvia. There was a tall, blond, blue-eyed German in charge of unloading us from the truck. He was a typical purebred Nazi, but he had only one arm, which is why he was working there. When I jumped down from the truck, he said to me, 'What are you doing here?' I said, 'What do you mean? I'm a Jew.' 'No,' he said, 'you don't belong there. You stay with me. You're not going anywhere.' Maybe he thought I was pretty and wanted to keep me as his girlfriend, give me good food for a while, then kill me or send me somewhere else. I looked him right in the face and said, 'I hate you. I hate every one of you. I will never stay with you. You can kill me this minute.' He could easily have shot me on the spot, but he just stared at me, then shoved me together with the others.

"What can I tell you about the camp that you don't already know from your own experience? It was terrible, overcrowded, scary. The Germans rushed back and forth shouting insults. They took everything we possessed and gave us a cold shower. They gave us other clothes that didn't fit. They threw the shoes at us. There were German women officers in the showers. They were just as cruel as the men, maybe worse. They acted like you were their personal enemy, like you did something terrible to them. They just hated Jews, you could see the hatred in their faces.

"Early in the morning it was so cold. We'd have the roll call, and we'd be out in any kind of weather, half-naked. They would count and count us. Sometimes they sent us to other camps, at first just to concentrate the Jews. From there, they took some out and killed them. If they were a little older or couldn't work so much or walk so fast, or if they didn't like your face, they shot you on the spot. They called that a selection. I was lucky. I was taken to a series of work camps.

"In one of these camps, they made parts for big German boats. We made something like a big, black, oval, inflated tire. Not all the Germans were completely bad. There was one worker who tried to help us. He wasn't allowed to talk to Jews, but he would put a sandwich by the big machine where I worked. As hungry as I was, though, I would never take it. I finally told him, when no one else was around, 'Don't bring any more sandwiches. I will not be helped by a German.' That was my pride, Henyu. But I was very, very hungry. I was starving.

"I had quite a few friends in the camps, Poles and Czechs mostly. Once I was terribly sick with some kidney infection. When somebody got sick, they sent them to a make-believe hospital and then, periodically, they would empty the hospital and kill everyone there. If you couldn't work, you were no good to them. So my friends hid me on the top bunk and covered me with blankets. I was so skinny that my body didn't stick out much. I didn't even want to eat anything, but they forced me to have some of their soup. In the morning, I had to stagger out to the roll call to be counted. Eventually I got better and went back to work.

"In another work camp, I had the best job you could have, in the kitchen. I sat all day peeling potatoes. I didn't have to walk around, which was good, because I was so weak from being undernourished. Also, I got a little bit more soup, maybe, or an extra bit of bread. The only bad thing was that I cut my finger practically to the bone. See? I still have the scar. Nobody bothered with it. I just tied a piece of rag around it. I wouldn't even tell anybody because if they knew I had an infected finger, out I'd go.

"We were allowed cold showers, and I took advantage of them, even in the winter. Not everyone did. I wanted to be clean. I once gave a piece of bread, my whole portion for the day, for a piece of soap. I would fall frequently because I was so tired, but still I would try to wash my face and keep myself clean. I brushed my teeth with my finger. One day I asked if somebody had an onion. I don't know why. My body probably craved for the vitamins. So I traded my bread for a raw onion.

"They never kept us long in any one camp. The worst thing was when they started liquidating a place. As long as you were at a camp, you knew you were more or less safe for the time being. But when we moved, there would be a long line of Germans on both sides with machine guns. Every time they moved us, we thought, 'This is the end. Now we're going to be killed.' And of course many people were killed. Like when they took us to the concentration camp, Stutthof. They took us in cattle cars and trucks, all squashed like sardines together. In the very beginning, there were children who cried, and later, there were no children or older people, but people dying from hunger, dying from suffocation.

"For quite a while, I managed to keep with me a very strong poison from the lab in Vilno. It made me feel good, because I thought, 'If worse comes to worst, I can always kill myself.' At least I had the choice. Later on, I lost the poison and there was no choice.

"The thing I missed most was freedom, freedom from being told what I can and cannot do. I had never experienced that kind of pressure all the time, that fear. I thought often about my childhood and how it used to be before the war. I missed you, Henyu. I missed my parents a lot. We were so close. I prayed that they were all right. Many times, I thanked God that they were not with us in that camp.

"One day I heard that you were in the same camp, Henyu. I could not even see you because men and women were completely separated there. We got one piece of bread and some watery soup for the whole day. Some people separated this bread into two or three pieces and left some for later. I ate all mine right away. I was always hungry. But when I found out you were there, I asked one of the *Kapos* to give you my bread and soup. I didn't have anything all day, but it didn't matter. Now I find that you never got the food, you had already left that camp. Oh, well!

"Near the end of the war, we were taken to a labor camp attached to a factory in Magdeburg. For weeks there were rumors that the Americans were close. Then one day we heard planes going over, and someone said, 'Those are not German planes; they are American planes.' And I just prayed, 'Oh, please, throw the bombs right here, right here on top of all the Nazis.' I didn't think about myself, I just hated them so much.

"It was a gloomy morning, and I had a feeling that there was something wrong — that something bad was going to happen. The Germans were walking around the camp, gathering in small circles, whispering among themselves. Then they announced that we were being moved to a new camp. 'Don't be scared,' they said. 'We're going to another working camp, a good camp, a good camp.' They reassured us not because they were humane and wanted us to feel better, but to avoid any panic. They didn't want any extra trouble. They wanted everybody to go to their deaths in nice, even, two-by-twos. So they were moving people out of the camp a few groups at a time.

"But somebody got away and came back to tell us that not far away there was a river, and that the Germans weren't taking us to another camp, they were taking everybody to this river and killing them all, one by one. The Elbe River was red with blood. And the Germans were taking more and more people.

"I decided I was not going like a lamb to be killed. I was going to run — even if I was killed on the spot. I was so frightened, but I was also determined not to go to death without at least trying to escape.

"I had befriended Hanka, a Polish girl who was maybe a year younger than me. We became very close, and I felt kind of protective of her. I told her my plan and said, 'Listen, I'll hold your hand all the time while they lead us to this river, and when I tell you, "Run," we will both run. If they kill us, they kill us, but at least we run.' She was scared but she said OK.

"We didn't have to wait long. The same morning the orders came over the loudspeakers to leave the camp and the Germans started shouting *'Raus! Mach schnell!'* and searching in every building, in every corner, under every bunk. People gathered in long lines, and the Nazis, with their unfeeling, implacable faces, guarded us on both sides of the lines, their machine guns facing us. We were holding on to each other, my friend and I, and we were scared.

"Soon we started to move. The Germans were pushing and shouting, shouting, shouting. Some of the people were crying, some praying, and others were resigned to their fate.

"As we were walking, I kept asking one soldier near us: 'Listen, I don't mind dying, but tell me the truth. Where are you taking us? Are you taking us to our death?' He said, 'No, you are going to a beautiful, warm place and you'll get food and you're going to work for the German Reich. Don't worry, don't worry.' So I held Hanka's hand, and we walked and walked and walked. Some people fell because they were so tired, and they were shot.

"Finally, I decided: That's it, it cannot be that far. So I pulled Hanka's hand and whispered, 'Run, now! Run, run.'

"When we ran, the lines started falling apart. Everybody took off in different directions and the Germans started to run after us, shooting and shouting, *'Verflucte Juden! Dirty Jews!'* We heard a constant barrage of machine guns. People were falling like flies. 'Don't look back,' I said, and we didn't. We just kept running, running, running, expecting any moment to fall but, somehow, we didn't fall.

"We ran, all out of breath, past bombed out buildings, dodging around piles of rubble. Then, we came to a street with some houses, and ran inside a little courtyard, surrounded by three apartments. I saw a sign that said 'Laundry,' and we went in. There were these tremendous kettles and dirty clothes piled up, and some laundry hanging from a line. We hid behind one of the kettles. We heard shouting and machine guns for a long time. Several soldiers came into the courtyard, shouting and shooting in the air, but they didn't look in our laundry room. We sat there for many hours, behind the kettles, not moving at all. Finally, the shouting quieted down completely, and it was getting dark. I was shivering in a thin striped prison outfit, and I was afraid to go out looking like I did. Then, like a miracle, I saw a dress hanging up, a heavy, woolen, maroon knit dress. I felt as if God's hand had come down and He said, 'Go and you will be safe.' And I took it. Hanka found something, too. We washed our faces with some water from a kettle, and fixed our hair with wet hands so that we looked half-decent. Then we listened and listened.

"We walked out into the cold night and made our way towards the entry. There we saw an old man, a German, guarding the entry with a machine gun — not an SS man, but a soldier of the *Wehrmacht.* We stopped, not knowing what to do. Suddenly a fat woman came running out from one of the apartments. She was screaming that we were Jews and demanded that the guard kill us. He said quietly to the woman, 'You go inside. Don't worry. I'll take care of them. I don't want you to see what will happen. Just go inside now.'

"When she was gone, he told us, 'Listen. You run. I'm going to shout and I'm going to shoot over your heads. This is the end of the war. I want no more killing. The Americans are on the other side of that bridge. Just keep running, and don't be afraid. I will not kill you.'

"I didn't believe him, of course, but we started running, and he shouted and shot — du-du-du-du-du — but nothing happened. Nothing hit me in the back. And we ran to the other side.

"Just after we crossed the bridge, we saw big tanks and, as we got closer, these big brown boots. Then I looked up, and saw the American soldiers sitting on the tanks. They looked beautiful — like angels from heaven. One soldier got down, and I hugged him. I had always told myself that if Americans ever liberated us, I would kiss the first soldier. But I was too bashful.

"I couldn't believe what was happening. We were so scared, and they were so friendly, with their outstretched hands and the feeling of welcome in every word they said. I could understand them, you know, because my mother made me study English before the war. And they gave us cheese and bread and some delicious chocolates. We ate everything. We were lucky, because some people like us were not used to the food, and they got sick and died.

"Soon after that I got very sick. I got an infection in my left leg. It was full of pus. Then it spread to the other leg, and I couldn't walk for months. They took me to a hospital located in a Polish DP camp. I had a terribly high temperature, and the doctors thought nobody could live through that. But I did.

"Everybody thought I was Polish. They didn't know I was Jewish. There was an American doctor who liked me a lot. He kept telling me that he would take me to his mother because he wanted to marry me. I kept trying to tell him I was already married, but I didn't know the English word. So I said, 'I already have a man.' And he said, 'You mean you already have a husband.' And I said, 'No, no, I don't have a husband.' I thought 'husband' was some disease. Oh, that was so funny. Finally, he understood, but he continued to be very friendly and helpful.

"I had a lot of time to think about what had happened to us while I was sick, Henyu, about what happened to all the Jews. You know I am a person who has always believed in people, in their essential goodness. I still do, even after what we've been through. I believe in the goodness of the human soul. But I hate the Nazis. It's something I cannot get over, and I don't know if I want to get over. They killed everyone in my family, everyone in your family. I know them. I know them well.

"Yet I know some Germans were good. There was that soldier, the old German who let us run. He was a good man. And there were a few others. I thought about all of this, trying to sort it out, but I could not.

"Slowly, I got better. An officer who was a liaison between the Polish DP camps and the American authorities asked me to work in the office in the camp. I couldn't walk yet, but there was a nice young Polish man who had a bicycle, and he would carry me on the handlebars to the office so that I could work.

"I gradually learned to walk again. Then I was approached by an UNRRA officer who was coming to the Polish camp. He asked if I would like to work as a translator. Of course I agreed, and that's how I started working for UNRRA. That gave me the possibility to look for you, Henyu. I found out that there were central offices where you could send letters with names of people one was looking for. So I sent letters all over, asking about you.

"My boss was a Dane, Major Christensen, who became my close friend. One day, I came to the office and he said that there was a letter for me. I couldn't believe it. They said that there was news that Henry Lilienheim was alive. I kept reading and reading it, thinking, 'Maybe it's another Lilienheim. Maybe this is a mistake. I shouldn't get my hopes up.' Then I wrote back. And you got the letter, and here we are.

"It still seems like a miracle to me, Henyu, that we have both survived and found each other. I will never let you out of my sight again."

The Album

AS EVENING SETTLES, Lydia and I decide to stop overnight at an inn in the town of Fulda. While we are having dinner, a thought flashes through my mind. The chief of the hospital in Vilno once told me he came from Fulda. The innkeeper is serving coffee. "Do you by any chance know a Dr. Boekamp?" I ask. "Oh yes," he answers. "He lives a few blocks from here."

The next morning we drive to the address the innkeeper has given us. It is a private home with a small garden. I ring the bell. Dr. Boekamp, a portly grey-haired man, answers the door. He is still in his bathrobe. He stares in amazement at Lydia and me.

"*Unglaublich!* Unbelievable!" He seems somewhat uneasy at the sight of our American uniforms.

"Dr. Boekamp," I say. "Excuse us for knocking on your door without warning. We happened to be passing through Fulda and thought of you. We've come to visit because we always respected you. We know you are a decent man, and we are not here to accuse you of anything."

"Please come in," Dr. Boekamp responds. "I'm sorry for staring," he says, more relaxed. "It's just so extraordinary to see you! I'm so glad you both have survived and that you look so well."

We answer all of Dr. Boekamp's questions about our experiences in the camps. He is very sympathetic and obviously feels guilty for the horrors in which he played a reluctant role. We talk about people who worked in the hospital, and I recall the Catholic nuns whom he protected from persecution.

"Did Lieutenant Schmidt survive?" Lydia inquires. He was a particularly nasty Nazi who made life miserable for all the Jews and Poles at the hospital.

"No," Dr. Boekamp replies, "and I cannot say it disturbs me. He fell in action back at the front. But, please, excuse me a moment. There is something I must show you."

He leaves the room and comes back with an album in his hands. "This is the only thing I salvaged from the war," he says, handing it to me. Inside I see the familiar red and black letters in medieval German script:

> As sure as May comes every year,
> The time will come when this storm is over.
> Years later you will think of the war
> And remember the places you once were.

It is one of the albums I had made five years earlier to barter with the German nurses and officers for food. My verse strikes me as bitterly ironic after all we have been through.

"As much as I value this album, you can have it if you wish," Dr. Boekamp says.

"No, it is yours, I made it for you."

Dr. Boekamp introduces us to his wife, a bosomy, grey-haired German matron. She wears a neat dress and a white lacy apron. She serves us strudel with coffee and cream.

"Das ist ja wie in einem Roman. It is all like in a novel," she says.

We spend about an hour talking and eating. The doctor talks about the pressures he worked under. "I hope you can understand," he says. "I knew that the Nazis were murdering innocent people, but if I protested overtly, I would only have been killed. So I tried to treat the Jewish laborers in a kind way, and help whenever I could. Should I have refused to minister to the soldiers because I was against what they were doing? Yet they were human beings, too, and I was trained as a healer. So I tried to do the best job I could for my patients. I often wonder if I did the right thing. I just don't know."

We tell him something about what it was like for us trying to survive in those days, living in the ghetto, being on guard every moment. Lydia reveals how she broke as many laboratory slides and dishes as she could in the hospital, trying to subvert the Nazi system in whatever small way she could.

Finally, there is an awkward silence. Even though we have reached across the gulf that naturally separates us, we can never feel completely comfortable with one another. Too much unspoken horror lies between us.

"It's time to leave," I finally say. "We still have to drive another four or five hours to reach Munich tonight." We shake hands.

As we drive away, Dr. Boekamp and his wife stand in front of their door, waving and calling: *"Auf Wiedersehen. Auf Wiedersehen!"* Lydia waves back, then turns to me and says, "So after all this cataclysm, we part like human beings."

We drive on as the sky becomes brilliant with the reds and oranges of the setting sun, then fades to a deep blue as night gently envelops the world. *L'heure bleue.* Lydia falls asleep, lulled by the hum of the Fiat. I think about everything that has happened in the past few days, how strange fate is, how easily everything could have turned out differently.

How incomprehensible is the mystery of the universe. I am obsessed with the question of reality. Were the events of this day real or am I dreaming? Will I wake up in a moment to find myself in a concentration camp with smoke spewing from the chimneys of the crematoria?

No, I am not dreaming. As I drive, Lydia sleeps beside me. In her lap she is holding her stuffed mascot, the black cat. I think of Dr. Boekamp. Not so long ago, one word from him meant life or death. This afternoon, when he opened the door and saw us in American uniforms, there was fear in his eyes. Then, later, he brought out the album with my German verse. If someone had suggested when I was writing that verse that some day Lydia and I would visit Dr. Boekamp in Fulda, I would have found the thought preposterous. But the unthinkable has happened.

And now we are driving into our future. We will put back together the shards of our broken lives. Soon, I hope, we will leave Germany. Here there is a constant ache in my heart that keeps me from being truly alive. I am sure that when I leave Germany, my heart will beat normally once again. I will be able to respect older people, build new friendships, admire beautiful women, play with children in a park. I dream of moving to America, the land of the liberators, the home of freedom.

I inhale the fresh, invigorating night air.

Homelessness

LYDIA AND I settle into our life together in my Munich apartment overlooking the tree-lined canal. We begin to build our marriage again, out of the ruins of the past.

We spend a lot of time talking about the war, our families, the friends we miss. We take long walks, go often to films, and picnic on the grounds of the nearby Nymphenburg Palace, enjoying the expanse of green grass, the insects and birds. Sometimes we drive to the mountains for a holiday, and eat black bread washed down with fresh, whole milk.

Our bodies have made a miraculous recovery, after what we have endured. Lydia's leg is completely better, and I have regained almost all my strength.

Our spiritual wounds have not healed, but these beginnings are full of promise for us. We are survivors, favored by fate. In the aftermath of this great storm, we can still walk in the warmth of sunshine and life.

I return to my work for the U.S. Military Government. I also have another job. The Government of Bavaria has formed a special Department for Jewish Affairs, and the chief of the Department asks me to assist him in an advisory capacity. I also work part time in the public relations office of the Joint Distribution Committee, a Jewish-American organization to help survivors with their many needs and problems.

Although our lives have returned to a semblance of normality, Lydia and I long to leave Germany. Our intense desire is shared by the great majority of Jewish DPs. It overshadows all other concerns. Most of the Jews do not want to adjust, even temporarily, to life in Germany.

The only solution is emigration, but even after the cruelty of the Final Solution, Jews still face an indifferent world. Many Jews, especially the young, want to go to Palestine, but the doors are closed to them. The doors of the United States are only slightly open, and a few slip through, while the debates continue in America over President Truman's humanitarian efforts.

Homelessness. By a bitter twist of fate, Jewish children are being born on German soil. Is there no place under God's sun for the survivors? Was the greatest tragedy in the history of the Jewish people, I wonder, just another event in the chain of suffering?

Anti-semitism surfaces again. There seems to be no repentance among the Germans for the crimes committed against other nations and, particularly, against the Jews. If the opportunity arose again, the crimes would probably be repeated with the approval, or silent acquiescence, of the majority. I am amazed to read a letter sent to the Jewish Committee in Garmisch from a German Hausfrau:

> In the course of this week, I have had the opportunity to visit Garmisch and Mittenwald. I was amazed at how many Jews one can see in this country, a part of Germany where no Jew could be seen before. I have concluded that the allegation that the Jews were liquidated

in concentration camps is false, or else all these creatures who are alive have risen from the dead.

Before the war, I knew many Jews; nearly all of them are still living. I could locate all but one or two. I feel a great disgust and hatred toward this race who carries the guilt for the misery in Europe and Germany. Why do they come back in such masses? This is shameless. These people will not escape from a well-deserved punishment.

Fortunately, this letter does not represent the feelings of all Germans. A more encouraging editorial appears in a Frankfurt newspaper, quoting the apostle John, "He who hates his brother is a murderer," the article begins. "We cannot give life back to the six million Jews who were murdered," the writer continues, "but we can change our attitude from one that is still unfriendly to one of understanding and compassion."

I know that this represents a minority German viewpoint, as the interviews I conduct in my work reveal. I engage an automobile mechanic in conversation. "We never liked the Jews," he tells me, "but we only started to hate them during the early years of the war, when we were ordered to. After the catastrophic surrender, there was no more hatred against the Jews, but that only lasted about half a year. Today, we hate them again. You see, life is hard. We live in misery, and the Jews, it seems, enjoy better conditions of life."

It is becoming more and more difficult for me to listen to such sentiments. I want to scream at him, to tell him what it was like in Dachau, to ask him if he would "enjoy" knowing that his family had all been killed. But I don't. I simply listen and record, letting them damn themselves with their own words and hatred.

Kaddish

"*BE CAREFUL,*" *Dworzecki says.* "*The* Kapo *is coming.*"
I dig the earth. It is grey, grey as the color of my skin.

When the kapo *moves away, I say to Dworzecki,* "*I don't know what's happening to me today. I have been dreaming the whole day.*"

"*It's been an easy day,*" *he says.* "*Not too cold. The work isn't heavy and our rations weren't bad.*"

"*Did we reach seven hundred calories?*" *I ask.*

Dworzecki calculates. "*No, about five hundred and fifty. But with the soup tonight, we should reach six hundred and fifty.*"

"*Listen,*" *I say after a while.* "*Imagine that someone tells you that you will be born again, that good fortune will give you everything — health, looks, wealth, intelligence, success — that you will travel and see the world and enjoy every minute of your life for another sixty years. But, like Faust, you will have to pay for all this with four years of the suffering we are going through. Would you accept such a proposition?*"

"*No,*" *Dworzecki replies without hesitation.* "*No one of sound mind would accept it.*"

"Why, then, do we stick so stubbornly to our hope for the remaining years of our lives? Can those years compensate for all this?"

Dworzecki considers my question. "It's a blind instinct, the will to live," he answers. "We know only one thing, survival. We believe that the war will end soon and we will be free. We couldn't live without that hope; it keeps us alive from day to day. If we had known at the beginning what was in store for us and how long it would last, wouldn't we have given up the battle long ago?"

"But has our suffering any meaning?" I continue. "Is there any compensation for our struggle? And what does the future hold?"

"For me it is Palestine," replies Dworzecki. "But we have neglected our Hebrew lesson today. If we have a good day tomorrow, we will have the next lesson. You must know Hebrew so that you can say Kaddish, the Prayer for the Dead."

Silence. We keep digging.

Yes, I think. I will have to say Kaddish. I will have to say Kaddish.

Birth

THE TREE IN FRONT of our apartment window changes its cloak. The buds open, and the branches are covered with leaves. In the canal across the road, the water shimmers in the sunlight. I gaze with delight at the symphony of colors. Green leaves, blue water, azure sky and white clouds. Month after month I observe the rhythmic cycles of nature. Soon the leaves will turn yellow and fall to the ground. The wind will heave them into the air and toss them on the water. The trees will become naked, and the sky grey. As I watch Nature changing, I understand that every living being is a link in the chain of existence. Each being comes into the world, lives, grows, and passes away.

I often walk along the canal, searching my mind for answers to the puzzle of life. But the answers are so difficult to find. I understand that we live in the darkness of our ignorance, with only pale lights flickering here and there. The future, perhaps, will reveal more lights, but these lights will never dispel the darkness. Neither philosophy nor the progress of science can explain the mystery of existence.

My heart desires God, but if He exists, I cannot find Him or understand His ways.

What is the cause of unhappiness and misery? I ask myself. Hatred. What gives us happiness and desire for life?

Love. Love for a mother, for a woman, for a child. Love for people and ideals.

And what is morality, I ask myself. It must be the judgment of one's own soul, one's sensitivity to another's suffering, one's action in response to that suffering.

Yet how sick and cruel people can be. What dark forces hide under the thin veneer of "civilization." We have changed so little through the ages. Sometimes, in the company of people, I imagine them in the zebra-striped clothes of the inmates in the camps. How would they behave? Would they act like hungry beasts, or would their humanity shine through? In the company of Germans, I often mentally clothe them in SS uniforms. I try to see through the superficial layer of polite manners. Over and over, I hear the inevitable declarations: *"Ich war immer dagegen. Ich als alter Gegner der Nazis.* I was always against them. I am an old anti-fascist." Show me your real face, I think.

What has the war accomplished? True, civilization was saved by destroying Nazism. But our expectations are now so great. Perhaps too great. I read in the papers: "Atomic bombs could wipe out great cities and create poisonous radioactive clouds which would sweep around the world, raining slow and unseen death on every living being." I cannot help wondering: What would have happened if Hitler's scientists invented that bomb? What will happen when a future *Führer* arises with such power at his fingertips?

"You do not love humanity," President Wilson said after World War I, "if you seek to divide humanity into jealous camps. Humanity can be welded together only by love, by sympathy, by justice, not by jealousy and hatred." Naive, I think, yet so beautiful. I only wish I could believe that such a unity may happen some day.

I open the Book of Prophets. I read from Jeremiah, that angry, tortured soul. Like me, he asks the bitter questions, calling God to account, yet longing for His entry into his soul. In the music of Jeremiah's words, I find the reflection of my own deepest feelings:

> He hath led me, and brought me into darkness. He hath made my chain heavy.
>
> He hath covered himself with a cloud, that our prayers should not pass through.
>
> Mine enemies chased me sore, without cause.
>
> And I said, my strength and my hope is perished from the Lord.
>
> My soul hath still in remembrance mine affliction and my misery, and is humbled in me.
>
> The Lord is my portion, saith my soul; therefore will I hope in Him.
>
> O Lord, thou hast seen my wrong: judge Thou my cause.

I do not know whether God ever answered Jeremiah to his satisfaction. I am still waiting for His reply.

The first snow has fallen, and everything is white. The pendulum of time moves rhythmically. My wife has borne a child. As I bend by the bed of my little daughter, I do not know whether I love her. But when she smiles for the first time, my heart is filled with sweet feelings.

As I look at her, it seems to me I see my mother, my father, my sister, my little niece. I see Lydia's parents. I see a reflection of myself. Our child has come into the world because we did not perish in the camps, and one link has given hand to another.

Afterword

LYDIA AND I have come from our home in Glencoe, a suburb of Chicago, to celebrate my 85th birthday. Our daughter Irene has organized a party with speeches and entertainment by our friends. Some seventy guests are coming, including many from various cities.

It is early evening. The guests will arrive in two hours. I relax in an easy chair looking out the big window of the living room. I see the lovely park along Esplanade Avenue. In the background, Mount Royal rises with its illuminated cross on the top. City lamps cast a silvery shine. It has been a long journey in more ways than one to come to this spot.

My thoughts wander to the past, over a span of close to half a century, from the time the second part of my life began. I did not really expect to survive the camps. I could have died there, never to have seen Lydia again, never to have fathered my two children. As I think back, I realize that I have been graced.

I see the faces of my family and friends, now long gone. My heart longs for them. My mother and father sit down to dinner with Maurice, Edwarda, Szymon, little Misia and me, back in our apartment in Warsaw. Ignas appears, beaming with life, and challenges me to a game of tennis. Marek Dworzecki faces me, his deep, melancholy eyes once again conveying eloquent silence. After his sojourn in Paris, he did move to the new state of Israel, where he practiced medicine and continued to write.

Perhaps I think about the past so much because Irene has convinced me to knock the dust off of my old manuscript, *The Aftermath*. She has rediscovered it and helped in the editing. In large measure, I wrote it as a gift for her, just after her birth. I wrote it in English, rather than in Polish, because I planned all along to raise my children in America.

As I sit here and look out the window, I remember the day in 1949 when Lydia and I landed in New York with our two-year-old, Irene. I recall the struggle to adjust to a new life, to a new country. I apprenticed in the office of a patent lawyer in New York as a technical draftsman and translator, while Lydia worked in a medical laboratory. Then we moved to Chicago, where I worked during the day and attended law school at night. With my prewar French engineering degree and my new American degree in law, I embarked on a career as a patent attorney. For a short time I worked as a lawyer in Geneva, Switzerland and Turin, Italy. Eventually, I also organized my own international company for the transfer of technical know-how and the manufacture of licenses, and opened thirty offices around the globe. It was an interesting life. Lydia and I made frequent trips to many countries. Our son, Michael, was born and grew to be a kind, empathetic young man. Irene grew to become a lovely woman, and a gifted filmmaker. Now she and her husband, Abbey, a talented film director, are hosting my birthday party.

I have nearly learned, after so many decades, to be humble. In my search for knowledge, I came to understand that what we acquire is only a drop in the ocean. The human mind is not equipped to solve the mysteries of existence: Whence do we come? Why were we created? Are we only a conglomeration of atoms which will disintegrate and vanish into nothingness, like snowflakes which fall into a river, only to evaporate and join the clouds again? Or is there an intelligence which rules the universe? If there is not, whence comes the voice within us which reminds us of the golden rule, which tells us to be kind and compassionate?

And why does that dark cloud cast a shadow which makes people kill one another in the name of progress, of racial purity, for the greater glory of God? What is the source of this evil? A defect in the genes? Imbalances of the neurotransmitters that obscure the mind and makes people indifferent to the sufferings of others? Or is sadistic cruelty simply a part of human nature?

My train of thought is interrupted by the sound of greetings. The first guests arrive. I return to the present.

The birthday celebration evokes overwhelming feelings of warmth and friendship. Speeches, recitations of poems, songs. I am grateful, and somewhat embarrassed.

Irene approaches. "Dad, you should make a speech." I stand up and crack a few jokes. Then I begin my story:

"It was late at night, the time when stars begin to twinkle, as if talking with one another. I was in bed, reading *The Interpretation of Dreams* by Sigmund Freud. Dreams, he wrote, express our suppressed desires. My lids grew heavy as I contemplated his words. I fell asleep.

"In a dream, I saw myself ascending a very tall ladder until I came to a landing. An angel in a white robe was standing there in front of an ornate gate. This must be Gabriel, I thought. The angel spoke. 'Who are you, and what are you doing here?' I told him my name. He looked at his list. 'You are not on the list. You do not belong here.'

"I was distressed. 'You can't send me back,' I protested, 'after I climbed so high.'

"'It's useless to argue,' the angel replied. 'But I will do

something for you. I shall give you a gift to take back to Earth which will make your greatest dream come true.'

"I followed the angel and we reached another gate. He opened it, and we entered a small, round chamber. In the middle, on a marble-topped table, was a small mahogany chest. The angel opened the lid. I was dazzled by the sparkling radiance of many colors. 'Each of these rings has a different gem,' the angel said. 'You may take one. Inside the rim of each ring is an engraving which will tell you what the ring will give you. Take your time and choose carefully.'

"I picked up one of the rings. It was an emerald of a wonderful green color. Inside the rim was engraved the word 'Money.' Gosh, I thought, what I can do with this ring! I'll buy antique furniture, Louis Quinze commodes, a Renoir, perhaps *'Le Moulin de la Galette.'* I'll go on a safari to Kenya, stay in the world's best hotels — the Ritz of Paris, the Oriental of Bangkok, the Intercontinental of Karachi.

"But then I thought of the angel's admonition. There may be something more rewarding than money. I picked another ring with a bluish-green gem, the color of clear lake water. It was an aquamarine from Brazil. Inside the rim I read the word 'Beauty.' Beauty — the gratification of the ego, of vanity. I'll be as handsome as a Greek god, as beautiful as Michelangelo's David. I was about to decide on this ring when something cautioned me that such a choice would lead to only superficial satisfaction. Isn't beauty only temporary?

"I picked up another ring, and it seemed like I was holding a small star ready to explode into a thousand lights. It was a diamond from South Africa. The carved inscription read, 'Creativity.' Oh, God! To be creative. To be a poet, a novelist. To have a muse sit on my shoulder and whisper the right words in my ear. To know that what I write about my experiences will not be buried and forgotten in the sands of time.

"But something warned me that creativity may not be the highest value. There is more to life than to create. I picked another gem. It was a ruby from Burma, as red as the color of blood. Inside was engraved 'Health.' Ah, this is probably the greatest gift of all. You don't know how much to value health until you lose it. You can have money and beauty and be creative, but what is it worth if pain and weakness overpower you? Yet, once again, curiosity prompted me to hesitate. Maybe I was losing the opportunity to choose something even more valuable.

"I plunged my hand again into the chest and pulled out a ring with a gem of a yellowish-brown color. Amber. For millions of years, a mixture of the resin and oil of Baltic pines was washed by water, slowly transforming into this gem. Inside the rim of the ring were engraved the words, 'Peace of Mind.' Peace of mind, serenity, isn't this more important than health? You may be healthy, but without peace of mind, you will still be miserable.

"But is that all there is? I wondered. There must be something even greater than these gifts. I plunged my hand into the chest again.

"This time I found a ring with a lustrous, rosy gem. It was a pearl from the Persian Gulf. Long ago, a grain of sand entered the body of an oyster which then began gradually producing layers of nacre to protect itself against the invader. This resulted in tiny mineral crystals refracting light into the little rainbows that gave the pearl its wonderful iridescence. The suffering of the oyster produced this thing of great beauty, I thought. I remembered a poem by Alfred de Musset:

Mais qui sait comment Dieu travaille?
Qui sait si l'onde qui tressaille,
Si le cri des gouffres amers,
Si les eclairs et les tonnerres,
Seigneur, ne sont pas nécessaires
A la perle que font les mers?

Who can fathom the will of God?
Who can say if the raging waves,
The roar of the cruel deep,
The lightning's bolt,
The thunder's scream,
Are not necessary, O Lord,
For the sea to produce a pearl.

"I held up the ring with the pearl and read the words, 'Love and Friendship.' 'Yes!' I exclaimed. 'I have found it.' This was the ring I wanted. This was the greatest value. One can have all the advantages of the other rings, but life without love and friendship is meaningless, devoid of everything that warms and stirs the heart. Happy are people who share their life with others, who have warm relationships, who are married to a true friend. All other blessings pale in comparison to the gift of love and friendship.

"I chose the ring with the pearl."

March 8, 1993. Montreal.

About the author

The author in 1947, at the time of the writing of *The Aftermath*.

Henry Lilienheim, born in Warsaw, Poland, currently lives with his wife, Lydia, in a Chicago suburb. An essayist and poet, he speaks and writes nine languages. Lilienheim is also a retired textile engineer and international patent attorney. He and Lydia have a son and a daughter.

MARQUIS

PRINTED BY THE WORKERS OF
IMPRIMERIE D'ÉDITION MARQUIS
IN NOVEMBER 1994
MONTMAGNY (QUÉBEC)